OLD TESTAMENT
HISTORY OF REDEMPTION

BY

FRANZ DELITZSCH

TRANSLATED BY

SAMUEL I. CURTISS

HENDRICKSON
PUBLISHERS
PEABODY, MASSACHUSETTS 01961-3473

OLD TESTAMENT HISTORY OF REDEMPTION

Hendrickson Publishers, Inc. edition

ISBN: 0-913573-97-3

reprinted from the edition originally published
by T. & T. Clark, Edinburgh, 1881

First printing — April, 1988

Printed in the United States of America

PREFACE.

THE following manual of Old Testament History is one of Professor Delitzsch's four courses of University lectures on Biblical Theology. As such it has never been published in Germany. It is essentially an accurate reproduction of the paragraphs delivered to the theological students in Leipzig during the summer of 1880.

Although I was primarily moved to undertake this translation for the use of my students, yet I have found these lectures so stimulating and helpful in my own study of the Old Testament, that I venture to offer my rendering of them to the public, especially after the generous reception accorded to the *Messianic Prophecies* by the friends of Dr. Delitzsch in Great Britain one year ago.

SAMUEL IVES CURTISS.

LEIPZIG, *July* 28, 1881.

CONTENTS.

—o—

INTRODUCTION.

FIRST PERIOD.

FROM THE CREATION TO THE FLOOD. THE PERIOD OF THE PROTEVAN-
GELIUM, OR OF THE DAWNING OF THE LIGHT IN THE DARKNESS.

SECOND PERIOD.

FROM THE ELECTION OF ABRAM UNTIL THE EMIGRATION OF THE
FAMILY OF JACOB INTO EGYPT. THE PERIOD OF THE AGE OF THE
PATRIARCHS, OR OF THE SEPARATION AMONG THE NATIONS.

THIRD PERIOD.

FROM THE SOJOURN IN EGYPT UNTIL THE ARRIVAL IN SHILOH.   THE
    PERIOD OF THE DEVELOPMENT OF ISRAEL, AND THE SPRING-TIME
    IN THE LAND OF PROMISE.

FOURTH PERIOD.

FROM THE FOUNDATION OF THE KINGDOM UNTIL ITS DIVISION.   THE
    PERIOD OF DAVID AND SOLOMON, OR THE RISING AND SETTING OF
    THE ROYAL GLORY.

FIFTH PERIOD.

FROM REHOBOAM AND JEROBOAM I. UNTIL THE END OF THE DIVIDED
KINGDOM. THE PERIOD OF ISRAEL'S CONFLICTS WITH THE WORLD-
EMPIRES, AND OF PROPHECY, WHICH HOVERS OVER BOTH STATES
UNTIL THEIR FINAL CATASTROPHE.

SIXTH PERIOD.

SIXTH PERIOD.

CONTENTS.

SEVENTH PERIOD.

FROM JESUS' ENTOMBMENT UNTIL HIS RESURRECTION. THE
CONCLUDING SABBATH OF THE OLD TESTAMENT HISTORY.

OLD TESTAMENT HISTORY OF REDEMPTION.

INTRODUCTION.

§ 1. *Name.*

THE fundamental Biblical part of the entire theological system is throughout historic. The Old Testament half is divided into the history of the Old Testament literature; into the history of the contents of revelation as laid down in the Old Testament Scriptures, with its presuppositions; and into the history of the preparation for redemption up to the point where, after the foundation of redemption had been essentially laid, the old dispensation separates from the new. We shall devote our attention to this history of the preparation for redemption, or, what is the same, to the Old Testament history of redemption. We can also call it History of the Old Covenant, for it is a covenant which forms the basis and sphere of the preparatory history of Christianity, namely the Sinaitic; but we do not call it History of Israel, because the preparation for redemption had begun long before there

A

was an Israelitish people, and because it runs through the history of the people of Israel, without standing in necessary connection with all its externals and details.

REMARK 1.—The earliest treatment of the Biblical history is the *Historia Sacra* by the Gallic jurist Sulpicius Severus (d. after 406 A.D.). It is likewise a history of the church until the time of that author. It was customary up to the last century to make the history of the Old and New Testament the propylæa of church history; but Biblical history and church history must be kept separate, since they are severally the history of a foundation and of a development. Even the special treatment of Old Testament history for a long time retained the designation of ecclesiastical history (*historia ecclesiastica*), for example, the *Historia Ecclesiastica Veteris Testamenti*, by J. F. Buddeus (b. 1667, d. 1729), Halae 1715, and in many editions. Augustine (b. 354, d. 430 A.D.) has the broader conception of *civitas dei* for *ecclesia*. He wrote the *City of God* (*De Civitate Dei*, begun about 413, and not finished before 426), in twenty-two books. His conception of the city of God coincides with the idea of the kingdom of God. Hengstenberg (b. 1802, d. 1869), following his example, entitled his Old Testament history, *Geschichte des Reiches Gottes unter dem Alten Bunde*, 2 Bde., Berlin 1869–1871, "History of the Kingdom of God under the Old Covenant,"[1] etc. But the

[1] This work has been published by T. & T. Clark, in two volumes, with the title, *History of the Kingdom of God under the Old Testament*, Edinburgh 1871–1872.—C.

subject of Old Testament history is first of all the coming salvation,—compare John iv. 22, last clause: "For salvation is from the Jews,"—and then subsequently the form of that community, which it took on and which is its goal.

REMARK 2.—Roman Catholic theologians have given their text-books of Biblical history the title, History of the Biblical or Divine Revelation.[1] The idea of redemption could be easily combined with this designation, and then the title would be, History of the Old Testament Revelation of Redemption. But we do not adopt it; because (1) this name corresponds too little to the human as well as divine side of our task; and (2) this designation is contrary to New Testament usage, according to which the revelation ($\dot{\alpha}\pi o\kappa\dot{\alpha}\lambda\upsilon\psi\iota\varsigma$) of salvation is characteristic of the New Testament.

REMARK 3.—The name, History of the Old Covenant, would be just as fitting as the one chosen by us;[2] for the Sinaitic covenant is really the basis and periphery of the history of Israel to the point where, through the Risen One, the national barriers were broken down. The federal theology, founded by John Cocceius (b. 1603, d. 1669) in 1648 in Franecker, uses for this

---

[1] Thus, *e.g.*, Haneberg, *Geschichte der biblischen Offenbarung*, 3d ed., Regensburg 1863; and Danko, *Historia Revelationis Divinæ Veteris et Novi Testamenti*, Wien 1862–1867.

[2] This designation, *Geschichte des Alten Bundes*, has been adopted by Kurtz in his work, which still remains incomplete, Berlin 1848; and in the text-books of Hasse, Leipzig 1863; and of August Köhler, Erlangen 1875–1881, which has been finished as far as the time of David. The full title of this last work is, *Lehrbuch der biblischen Geschichte Alten Testaments*.

the expression *historia œconomiœ ante legem et sub lege;* but the conception of the covenant which contains law and promise relieves us of this twofold division, which is rather dogmatic than historic.

REMARK 4.—Old Testament history has been treated under the title, *Geschichte des Volkes Israel,* "History of the People of Israel," by Ewald[1] (b. 1803, d. 1875), by Hitzig[2] (b. 1807, d. 1875), and by Wellhausen[3] (b. 1844). But we reject this title, for Israel is not the goal and proper object of our historiography, but the salvation which existed before Israel had a being, and the covenant which gave Israel more than a national significance.

§ 2. *Presuppositions.*

Without claiming to be destitute of presuppositions, we acknowledge at the very start, that in our future narrative of the Old Testament preparation for the essential salvation we set out with three presuppositions. We presuppose (1), in general, that we have in the Old Testament Scriptures an authentic monument, a sufficient and an essentially harmonious document, of the course of Old Testament history. (2) That this history is not merely a part of the history of the civilisation of mankind by means of an absolute self-development, but a history going forth from God and

---

[1] This work, which has been published in several editions in Göttingen, first began to appear in 1843, and was finally completed in 1859. The second edition of the English translation was issued in London, 1871.

[2] In two parts, Leipzig 1869.   [3] Vol. i., Berlin 1878.

man as factors, which aims particularly at the re-establishment of the fellowship which was intended in the creation of man, and which was lost through the corruption of the intellectual and moral nature. (3) Since such a history is not possible unless the free activity of God and of man interpenetrate, we presuppose the reality of miracles, whose general character consists in the interference of the free will in the mechanism of nature as ordered by law, and whose historical pledge is the resurrection of Jesus, with which not only Christianity, but in general revealed religion and the Biblical view of the world, in contradistinction from the modern, stands and falls.

REMARK 1.—(1) No miracles occur in the natural world in itself considered. It is a miracle of almighty power, but after it has once been created, all in it is natural.

(2) History is the realm of the miraculous. The relation of God to free beings involves interferences in the course of nature, which make it serviceable for definite ends.

(3) The essence of the miracle is the impulse, and the chief thing is the result. The medium between impulse and result is the subjugated process of nature. The laws of nature are not set aside, but their working, in order that that which has been willed may be attained, is forced in certain directions, and is either checked or hastened.

(4) The course of the natural order of the world suffers a change, because the workings of another world-

system, namely of the historical, ethical, and spiritual, interfere with its course. These two world-systems are equally divine, and God has placed them in a reciprocal relation, from the time when there was not only a natural world, but also free beings, that is, from the beginning of history.

REMARK 2.—The resurrection of Jesus Christ is the fact by which the standpoint for the comprehension of the course of Biblical history is decided. If this one miracle is granted, it must at the same time be granted that it is the conclusion of miraculous premises, and that it has miraculous consequences in its train. Hence all the more honourable is the confession of H. Lang (b. 1826, d. 1876): "As soon as I can persuade myself of the reality of the resurrection of Jesus Christ, I shall tear in pieces the modern view of the world."[1] And Alexander Schweizer raises the question with respect to the resurrection of Jesus Christ: "Ought, then, really, under the presupposition of this one fact, the entire modern view of the world to be given up?"[2]

§ 3. *Aim.*

If we set out from these presuppositions, we are certain that we shall not represent the materials of the Old Testament history as they may appear to our accidental subjectivity, but in accordance with the

---

[1] *Zeitstimmen aus der reformirten Kirche der Schweiz*, Winterthur 1861, p. 349.

[2] *Protestantische Kirchenzeitung*, Berlin 1862, p. 275.

sense and spirit of the Holy Scriptures, and of the sacred history itself; and only as we begin with these presuppositions will it be possible to reproduce the materials of the Old Testament history in such an inward, living, and harmonious way as is, according to Gervinus[1] and Droysen,[2] the highest aim of all historiography. For since we are certain that the Old Testament progress in the appearance of Jesus the Christ, and in the relation of God to man mediated through Him, has reached its goal, we also know, by putting ourselves back in this progress towards the goal, to which everything tends, what is of integral religious significance in it. We penetrate the idea which works through this progress to its accomplishment.

REMARK.—It must be acknowledged from every standpoint that Jesus is the Israelite in whom the religion of Israel has come to the realization of its world-wide calling. Hochstädter[3] (Rabbi in Ems) says that the merit of Jesus consists in His having denationalized the knowledge of the true God, and in His having made it the common property of the entire human race. If this be admitted, then He is throughout the entire Old Testament the One who is to come. He is the conclusion of all Old Testament premises.

---

[1] *Grundzüge der Historik,* Leipzig 1837.
[2] *Grundriss der Historik,* Leipzig 1868; 2d ed. 1875.
[3] See his *Religionsphilosophischen Erläuterungen,* Bad-Ems 1864.

§ 4. *Arrangement.*

If, now, we observe how the Old Testament history articulates itself, so far as we extend it to the Sabbath between the burial and resurrection of Jesus, as the exact end of the Old Covenant, we discover six steps, with which they tend toward the goal attained in the seventh.

(1) The primitive period before and after the flood, with the dawning of the light in the darkness, which began before the flood and was renewed after it.

(2) The period of the patriarchs, or the separation in the tumultuous sea of nations.

(3) The period of Israel's development, and its transplantation to the promised land.

(4) The period of David and Solomon, or the rising and setting of the royal glory over Israel.

(5) The period of Israel's conflicts with the world-empires, and the elevation of prophecy, which poises over both states until their fall.

(6) The period of the recognition, which breaks through in prophecy and chochma, of the Mediator and of the Logos, and the historical appearance of the Messiah, who is no longer conceived of in a one-sided way as national, but as human and spiritual.

(7) The death and burial of the One who has appeared, and with Him of the Old Covenant: the concluding Sabbath of Old Testament history.

The protevangelium marks the beginning of the first period; the call of Abram, the commencement of the second; the passage through the Red Sea, the commencement of the third; the anointing of David, the commencement of the fourth; the dissolution of the kingdom, the commencement of the fifth; the beginning of the prophecy of the passion, the commencement of the sixth; and the entrance of the great Sabbath of the passion-week, the commencement of the seventh.

REMARK.—The apparently poetical expressions used in the designation of the periods indicate the parallelism in which the hexahemeron stands to the six steps of Old Testament history, for this parallelism is probably something more than accidental. Both of the apostolic gospels presuppose this parallelism, since Matthew places the beginning of his gospel (i. 1), "The book of the generation of Jesus Christ" ($B\acute{\iota}\beta\lambda o\varsigma$ $\gamma\epsilon\nu\acute{\epsilon}\sigma\epsilon\omega\varsigma$ '$I\eta\sigma o\hat{\upsilon}$ $X\rho\iota\sigma\tau o\hat{\upsilon}$), side by side with Gen. v. 1 (according to the Septuagint), "This is the book of the generation of Adam;" and John begins his history of the redemption with the words (i. 1), "In the beginning was the Word," which is evidently a variation of Gen. i. 1; and the old ecclesiastical eschatology presupposes it, since it indicates the closing period of the world's history as a seventh day ($\dot{\eta}$ $\dot{\epsilon}\beta\delta\acute{o}\mu\eta$).

§ 5. *Sources.*

Our first and chief source is comprised in the twenty-four canonical books of the Old Testament. They all serve in a manifold way the design of God, which was directed to these Scriptures in their entirety, as a true and serviceable monument of the anterior history of Christianity. The literature of the Egyptian, Babylonio-Assyrian, and Persian monuments render a subsidiary service; the Phœnician is of less importance. The Old Testament Scriptures, with whose historical portions Josephus' *Antiquities* run parallel until xi. 7, break off at the point where the collision between Judaism and Hellenism begins, which, so far as it was external and hostile, is represented in a credible manner by the first book of the Maccabees. The reciprocal relation of religion and civilisation, which was the result of this collision, is indicated by such books as the Wisdom of Solomon, which appeared before the time of Philo, and in general by the Hellenistic literature, especially of the Jewish Alexandrianism. The preparation for Christianity did not come to a stand-still with the period of Ezra and Nehemiah. In the literature of the following age also, which forms the bridge between the last books of the Old Testament and the New, both in the Palestinian and the foreign literature, the footsteps of the coming Christ may be recognised.

FIRST PERIOD.

FROM THE CREATION TO THE FLOOD. THE PERIOD OF THE PROTEVANGELIUM, OR OF THE DAWNING OF THE LIGHT IN THE DARKNESS.

§ 1. *The Riddle of the Primitive Beginning.*

THE first and most decisive period of all, which comprises at least two thousand years (Gen. v.; xi. 10), dates from the creation of the world, and especially from the creation of the earth with the heavens which belong to it. At the very beginning of the whole creation stands the *tohu vavohu* (Gen. i. 2, "And the earth was waste and empty"), which is absolutely contrary to the formed and animated. This chaos swims, like the extinguished sediment of a fiery catastrophe,[1] in unrestrained waters, and above these waters darkness rests. Chaos, roaring waters, and darkness are Biblical correlatives of wickedness, and of the evil which proceeds from wickedness. This picture of the beginning of the creation is there-

---

[1] Compare Isa. xxxiv. 9; Jer. iv. 23-26: "I beheld the earth, and, lo, it was waste and empty; and the heavens, and they were without light. I beheld the mountains, and, lo, they were trembling, and all the hills were shaken. I beheld, and, lo, there was no man, and all the birds of heaven had fled away. I beheld, and, lo, Carmel was a wilderness, and all its cities were overthrown before Jehovah, before His fierce anger."

fore dreadful, and it is a riddle that the creation has such a dreadful beginning, a riddle which must be solved. Heathenism in its philosophy, in which it considers chaos or the *hyle* (ὕλη) as eternally existent, leaves this riddle unexplained. The restitution's hypothesis solves it, but in a fantastic way. The right solution lies in the relation of the being of God to that of the creature. God, in the creation of the world, creates, on the one hand, an image of His being; on the other, an undivine being, and hence one entirely different from Himself. The creation of the world, therefore, and especially of the earth, begins with a condition corresponding to its undivinity. It begins with pure matter, which is farthest removed from God and the spiritual; yet not to remain therein, but in order that it may be brought up gradually from that condition, so as to become conformed to the divine image which is concentrated in man.

REMARK 1.—We say at least 2000 years, for the periods indicated in the Hebrew text of Gen. v.; xi. 10, from Adam to the Flood, give only 1656 years, and in the Samaritan text only 1307, but in the Septuagint 2242, or according to the reading 187 instead of 167, as the year when Methuselah had a son, 2262. These differences in the mode of reckoning afford free play to historical investigation. The greatest widening rather than the narrowing of the chonological net is to be recommended.

REMARK 2.—The account of the creation begins (Gen. i. 1) with an all-comprehensive summary statement.

The creation which is here intended is the first begin-ning, which was not preceded by any other, hence the creation of the universe, which also embraces the heaven of heavens.   That which follows in the second verse is not an exhaustive specialization, but one con-fined to the earth and its heavens.

REMARK 3.—Since the Tora bases the legal com-mand for the observance of the Sabbath (Ex. xx. 11, xxxi. 17) upon the Sabbath of creation, the hebdomad is more for it than an accidental scheme, the account of creation is more than a myth, in which the historical is a mirror of the author's thoughts.   It is a tradition, probably one brought by the patriarchs from Babylon, which, as it now appears as a part of the Tora, has been purified by the critique of the Spirit of revelation from mythological additions, a product of retrospective prophecy, which is also con-firmed by the fact that, aside from the fundamental religious truths which it attests, the historical part of the narrative has essentially maintained its ground until the present day.

REMARK 4.—The kind of substance which composed the chaos remains undetermined, for its being covered with water is only the first step in its creative forma-tion and animation.   The passages, Isa. xxxiv. 9 and Jer. iv. 23–26, are favourable to Plutonic conceptions of the earth's origin.   The restitution's hypothesis considers the chaos as the deposit of a wrecked world, whose destruction was coincident with the apostasy within the spiritual world.   But this view is without

support in the Scriptures, and is also without support
in the cosmogonies of the nations, a fact which alone
renders it suspicious.   It is impossible to translate Gen.
i. 2, " Then the earth had become waste and empty."
This construction as an apodosis to the first verse is
syntactically impossible.   The examples, Gen. vii. 10,
xxii. 1, are not homogeneous.

§ 2. *The Consequences of this Original Beginning.*

We understand now (1) the character of the world
of the six days.   It consists of a mixture of two
principles, namely, according to Gen. i. 2, of the
tohu (chaos) and the Spirit of God, or of death and
life.   It was in its relative completion, according to
Gen. i. 31, very good, but it was not yet the glorified
world.

We understand (2) its history; for after both
principles were equally commingled a development
is introduced, ascending from this good beginning and
running out into glory.

We understand (3) the possibility of evil; for the
ascending scale of creative progress from darkness to
light, from a dead mass to spirit and life, involves the
possibility of a relapse into the wild, spiritless, material,
natural ground of the primitive beginning.

We understand (4) the work of freedom, which
consists in this, that the self-determining creature
raises the nature which it has received by creation
into the sphere of freedom, whose correlate is glory.

It is now (5) also clear what the end will be, toward which the superhuman power of evil will strive, if there is such a power. It will endeavour to plunge the world in part and as a whole into the *tohu* (chaos) out of which God brought it up to Himself.

(6) The consequences of the primitive beginning extend still further to the conclusion of the world's history, which will remove the relative commingling of light and darkness in an absolute separation. The course of the world's history between that good beginning and this intended goal has as its middle place the earth, and has here as its mover and medium man, the being who occupies a middle position between yonder world of pure light and the present mixed world.

REMARK.—(1) The present world is commingled of two principles—matter and spirit, death and life, light and darkness, wrath and love; yet these do not form an independent dualism, they are derived from God. He is the primal ground of all things.[1]

(2) A proportioning or a harmonious commingling (*temperamentum*) of the contrarieties was the end of the six days' work, see Gen. i. 31.

(3) The nature of evil is disharmony. Its Hebrew designation with רע is derived from the radical signification of cracking (*fragor*), and רשע from that of loosening and unreliability. Both designations indicate the nature of evil as the disturbance of the equi-

---

[1] Isa. xlv. 7: "I form light, and create darkness; I make peace, and create evil; I, Jehovah, make all these."

librium, as the dissolution of that which is harmoniously united.[1]

(4) Freedom of choice is freedom as the possibility of self-determination in favour of the one or the other principle. It becomes freedom of power when man chooses the good, and from that point rules the evil; or, to use a Latin expression, it is *libertas arbitrii* in distinction from *liberum arbitrium;* it is the liberty (ἐλευθερία) described in 2 Cor. iii. 17, second clause: "Where the Spirit of the Lord is, *there is* liberty." The correlative of this freedom is glory, Rom. viii. 21: " In hope that the creation itself also shall be delivered from the bondage of corruption into the liberty of the glory of the children of God."

(5) *Tohu* is in the Scriptures the synonym of אַיִן, destitution of reality and worth (Isa. xli. 29),[2] also of שֶׁקֶר, perhaps originally *rouge,* hence *deception, falsehood* (Isa. xxix. 21),[3] and is used as a designation of idolatry, that is, of apostasy from God, 1 Sam. xii. 21. For evil is like the *tohu* of the beginning, *nihilum privativum,* namely, desolateness and emptiness, without moral support and value.

(6) The sinful world finally falls subject to the powers of the *tohu,* darkness [2] and fire; [3] and the final

[1] Compare Isa. lvii. 20 : " For the wicked are like the troubled sea, when it cannot rest, whose waters cast out dirt and mud."

[2] Matt. xxiv. 29 : " But immediately, after the tribulation of those days, the sun shall be darkened, and the moon shall not give her light, and the stars shall fall from heaven, and the powers of the heavens shall be shaken."

[3] 2 Pet. iii. 7 : " But the heavens that now are, and the earth by the same word have been stored up for fire, being reserved against the day of judgment and destruction of ungodly men."

result of temporal history is that two worlds are separated from each other, namely the world of glory, in which there is no night, Rev. xxi. 25, and the world of damnation, which is at the same time everlasting darkness and everlasting fire.

§ 3. *The Creation of Mankind and its Consequences.*

From the account of creation, Gen. i. 1–ii. 4, and its supplement in ii. 5 sqq., we see—

(1) That the creation of the spiritual and corporeal world finds its completion in man. Nature and spirit are personally united in him; he is the crown of the creation, since he is the copula of two worlds, which have him, the embodied spirit, as the centre of their history.

(2) That the body of man was created before his soul. The body is not the product of the Spirit. Man finds himself in a body which he is to govern through his spirit, and to spiritualize.

(3) That man is created in an entirely different way from other beings. His body does not arise at God's command (*fiat*), but as formed by God; and his spirit does not arise as the individualization of the universal life of nature (*spiritus mundi*), but as an immediate inbreathing of God.

(4) That man is not only partially but entirely created in the image of God. Hence even in the peculiar totality of his being he is the image of God. He is, on the one hand, unlike God in this, that the

nature of his being is compounded, and hence dis-
soluble; but, on the other hand, he bears in the matter,
as well as the spirit, of which he is composed the
stamp of his divine origin, and of the elevation of
his destiny.

(5) That man was originally created as one. This
unity in the beginning of human history conditions
the unity of its character and the possibility of a
divine work which comprises humanity as a whole.

REMARK 1.—The pre-eminence of man does not
consist in his having a spirit of life (רוּחַ חַיִּים), which
is also a characteristic of the animals (Gen. vi. 17,
vii. 15); but in this, that the endowment of the
animals with the spirit is not a special creative act,
and that they at once, as a multitude of individuals,
enter into existence. Man, however, comes into
being in such a way that God, in the entire fulness
of His personality, breathes into the *nostrils* of the one
man the breath of life (נִשְׁמַת חַיִּים), that he may become a living soul (נֶפֶשׁ חַיָּה), in a manner corresponding
to the personality of God, or, as the first chapter of
Genesis says, in the image of God. The basis of His
divine image is His personality.

REMARK 2.—It is an experimental fact that there
is a relation of man to man which is elevated above
the sexual relation, and which must be the intrinsic
element in that relation, if it is to have more than
an earthly value, and hence that the sexual relation
can cease without the cessation of love which binds
mankind together. The first man, as one, stands as

a prophecy of the future on the threshold of human
history, as a prophecy of the second Adam, as a prophecy of humanity like the angels in the state of
glory (Luke xx. 36).

§ 4. *The Sabbath, the Primitive State, Paradise.*

Between the creation and the history of the world
the Sabbath stands as a dividing wall, which is not
only God's rest from the creation, but also His
acquiescence in that which is created. God rested
in the world in order that it might rest in Him.
This rest of God in it made its rest in Him possible,
and His entrance into this rest was the destined end
of the world's development. God rested in man, so
far as the essential attributes of man were in peaceful
harmony, which corresponded to the holy being of God,
and therefore satisfied the Creator. It was a good
beginning [1] of a glorious physical and ethical end to
be attained by means of such impulses. And man,
attaining glory for himself, was to conduct all nature
with himself to glory. Hence the trichotomy of man
(body, soul, and spirit) corresponds to a trichotomy of
the earth, the world, Eden, and the garden of Eden;
for as soul and body were destined to become pneu-
matic through the spirit (1 Cor. xv. 45 sq.), so Eden
and the world by means of man, starting from Paradise,

---

[1] Eccles. vii. 29 : " Lo, this only have I found, that God hath made
man upright : but they have sought out many artifices." Prov.
viii. 31 : " Rejoicing in the inhabited part of the earth : and my
delights were with the sons of men."

were to become paradisal. Beginning with him, the microcosm, the glorification of the macrocosm was to go forth in ever-widening circles.

REMARK 1.—The Septuagint, the Samaritan and Syriac versions read, in Gen. ii. 2, the sixth day instead of the seventh, but erroneously. The Sabbath is indeed not a creative work, but it is the completion of the entire work of creation. It is the wall of partition between creation and the history of that which is created. Since this Sabbath no new being has been created. It is the beginning and the end of the consummation of the creature, for the Sabbath of God has the Sabbatism of the creature as its goal.

REMARK 2.—Paradise is, as Photius (d. 890) says, προοίμιον τῆς βασιλείας, that is, the very first plan of the glorified world. Paradise, as conceived by later writers, is the paragon of all beauty.[1] The prophets paint the Messianic final period with paradisal colours. Isaiah [2] and the New Testament Scriptures speak of a Paradise in the world to come, and of a heavenly Jerusalem, whose descent to the earth is the antitypical restoration of Paradise.[3] Hence the progress

---

[1] Gen. xiii. 10: "And Lot lifted up his eyes, and beheld all the circuit of the Jordan, that all of it was well watered, before Jehovah destroyed Sodom and Gomorrah, like the garden of Jehovah," etc. Joel ii. 3, second clause: "The land before them is like the garden of Eden, and behind them like a waste desert," etc. Comp. Ezek. xxxi. 8, xxxvi. 35.

[2] li. 3: "For Jehovah shall comfort Zion: He will comfort all her waste places; and He will make her wilderness like Eden, and her desert like the garden of Jehovah." Compare Isa. xi. lxv.

[3] Rev. xxi. 2: "And I saw the holy city, new Jerusalem, coming down out of heaven from God, made ready as a bride adorned for her husband."

and end of the history of salvation are prefigured in their paradisiacal beginning. That human history began and will end paradisiacally is correlated with its sinless commencement and its sanctified ending. However lacking in development we may consider the condition of the first man to have been, which the Scriptures do not deny, we must certainly regard him as in a condition of childlike innocence. Even from this it follows that the natural world all around appeared to him paradisal. The condition of childish innocence is in itself paradisic, and the world around us never seemed so beautiful as when we were children.

§ 5. *The Creation of Woman and the Fall of Man.*

It was a preliminary condition of all progress that man should take a decided position through his own experience with respect to the antagonistic principles of good and evil. Abstinence from the enjoyment of the tree of death was designed to secure for him the knowledge of good and evil, which is a prerogative of the angels [1] and of God.[2] After this trial of human freedom was prepared, the divine wisdom hastens with the sexual differentiation of man; for if Adam had fallen in his single state, the possibility of his redemption would have been rendered questionable, and human history would have been at an end as

[1] 2 Sam. xiv. 17, second clause : " For as an angel of God, so is my lord the king to discern the good and the evil," etc.

[2] Gen. iii. 21, first clause : " And Jehovah God said, Behold, the man is become as one of us, to know good and evil."

soon as the threatened death had taken place.   Hence
the programmatic announcement, Gen. ii. 18,[1] has an
infralapsarian background.   When, therefore, Adam
beholds the woman, he sees in her the bodily satisfaction of the longing which had been excited in him
when he mustered the animals; but it is significant
that she first falls a prey to the animal and satanic
temptation, and draws her husband after her in her
fall.   This first sin was fateful.   It was not the apex
of all sin, but it became the root of all sins.   It was
the first act in which man, placed before a moral
alternative, actualized his freedom of choice.   And
this first act was a fully conscious transgression of the
well-known will of God, proceeding from unbelief in
the truth of the divine threatening, and from distrust
of the divine love which surrounded man with
paradisal abundance.   The entire following history
takes its form from this catastrophe of the beginning.
On its night-side it is ruled by three powers—by the
animal, by Satan, and by death; for sin, proceeding
partly from the flesh, partly from the egoity, is either
carnal or satanic; and all sin stands in a reciprocal
relation to death, which in consequence of the original
sin has become a cosmical power; this is the meaning
of Rom. v. 12 : "Therefore, as through one man sin
entered into the world, and death through sin; and
so death passed unto all men, through which all (ἐφ'
ᾧ, referring to θανάτῳ) sinned."

[1] "And Jehovah God said, It is not good that man should be alone ;
I will make for him a helper as his counterpart."

REMARK.—In the narrative of the fall it is not a point of the greatest importance whether we understand it literally or symbolically, but whether we consider the event which rendered the redemption necessary a historical fact or not. The externality of that which is related conceals realities whose recognition is not shut out by a symbolical or even mythical interpretation. Christianity, as the religion of redemption, stands and falls with the recognition of the historical character of the fall.

§ 6. *The Consequences of the Fall.*

The first consequence of the fall was shame. The nakedness of mankind is no longer the appearance of their innocence. Their corporeity has fallen from the dominion of the spirit. Their beholding has become a sensuous imagining, and the flesh excites their fleshly passions.

The second consequence is death. The life of man's spirit has withdrawn from communion with God, and is, as it were, destroyed.[1] The life of his soul, through this despiritualization, has lost all true life. The life of the body has fallen into a state of corruption. The nature of man's being has sunken back to its lowest basis, and, so to speak, to its chaos, that is, to dust; and the return to dust (iii. 19) is only the end of the process of dissolution which had begun long before.

---

[1] Jude ver. 19 : " These are they who make separations, sensual, having not the Spirit."

The third consequence is the perversion of the relation of the earth to man, and of man to it, which is
expressed by the curse upon the ground which from
this time on is in continual conflict with its appointed
master.   And since nothing takes place in the world
without its vibrations being transmitted to its utmost
limits, the universe, through the victory of the wicked
one, and the defeat of mankind, has, so to say, under-
gone a shock in all its parts.[1]   But the dark side is not
without a comforting bright side.   Man having been
drawn away, has fallen under the power of darkness,[2]
not as purely spiritual, but at the same time as a
sensuous being.   The darkness is not yet that of hell.
But he would sink deeper and deeper if the eternal
decree of redemption, which in general is the basis of
man's existence, had not begun to be realized in time.

REMARK 1.—The Hebrew word for shame is בּוֹשׁ,
which properly signifies *disturbari*, to be disquieted and
disconcerted.   Shame is the overpowering consciousness of a deranged inner harmony, of a disturbed
satisfaction with oneself.[3]

REMARK 2.—The punitive sentence is not מוֹת תּוּגְמָת
(*thou shalt be put to death*), but מוֹת תָּמוּת (*thou shalt die*).
It does not indicate an arbitrary punishment with death,
but the necessary consequence of the transgression ;
and not an instantaneous death, but a dying beginning

[1] Gen. iii. 17, second clause : "Cursed is the ground for thy sake,"
etc.
[2] Col. i. 13: "Who delivered us out of the power of darkness," etc.;
Eph. v. 8 : "For ye were once darkness," etc.
[3] See Delitzsch, *Die Psalmen*, vi. 11.

from that time.   Compare Hosea xiii. 1: Ephraim
offended and died, that is, he carried thereafter the
germ of death in himself.

§ 7. *The Dawning of the Light and the Protevangelium.*

The first steps of Jehovah Elohim, who seeks man at
eventide, are the first steps of God the Redeemer
towards the goal of incarnation, which is the fundamental restoration of the immanence of the divine love
in the world.   The penetrating call, " Where art thou ?"
was designed to bring man to himself.   That our first
parents hide themselves, is, on the one hand, a proof
that their sin is still far removed from a hardening of
their hearts ; but, on the other, that the flesh now forms
a dividing wall between them and God, which from
fear of the Judge they seek to make still more dense.
When now the judicial examination follows, the serpent
and the one whose instrument it was are cursed because
of the seduction, the earth is cursed because of man,
against whom it is turned into a means of wrath and
chastisement.   Man himself, however, is not cursed,
but in the midst of the curse the dawn of the promise
rises upon him.   The end of the creation of man, in
spite of the fall, is not to remain unfulfilled.   This is
what the primitive promise warrants ; it is the entire,
eternal decree of love which is sketched in this protevangelium.   The Man of Salvation is not yet named,
but He is the centre of the collective he, the individualization of the human race.   He is from this time

the centre of humanity, which crushes the head of the
serpent; and the faith of the fathers derived from this
centre of the promise and of the promised One the
strength of hope and of sanctification in the struggle
with the power of evil. Since Adam calls his wife
Eve (*Chavva*), he announces his faith in the promise; and
since God provides for the covering of man's nakedness,
He typically prefigures His atoning grace; for כִּפֶּר
is a synonym of כִּסָּה, and signifies covering of sin, so
that in God's sight it is as though it did not exist.

REMARK 1.——When it is said that the serpent is
chosen as a symbol of the seductive charm of the
earthly, the question arises why the serpent was chosen
for this purpose. Probably because for the ancients,
and even now for uncivilised peoples, it is a ghostly
and mysterious creature.   On this account it was
especially adapted to represent an earthly power of
seduction with an unearthly background, and this
unearthly background is, as revelation further makes
known, the evil which had burst into the world of
spirits before the fall of man. The old Babylonio-
Assyrian and Persian tradition shows that the
serpent is thus to be understood.   The Babylonio-
Assyrian tradition calls the dragon or the serpent
aibu, that is, enemy *par excellence*, and calls it *tiâmat*,
as that which has risen out of the abyss of the
chaos (תְּהוֹם); and the Persian tradition calls it the
creature of Ahriman, or considers it as Ahriman
himself in the form of the serpent. It is, indeed, not
irrational to suppose that there are free beings raised

above men, among whom one excelling the rest has
apostatized from God; and experience, at least the
apostolic, confirms the fact that we have not to con-
tend alone with flesh and blood, and that human sin
is capable of increase until it becomes superhumanly
evil or diabolical. Hence there is a deep significance
for the scale of human sin in the fact that man,
befooled by an animal, fell into the first sin, and that
the seducer, whose demoniacal deceit consisted in
speaking through the serpent, is that being, which is
called in John viii. 44, with reference to the fall, " a
liar and the father of it " (*i.e.* the lie).

REMARK 2. — The promise in Gen. iii. 15, last
clause, is, " He [the seed of the woman] shall crush
thee on the head, and thou shalt crush Him on the
heel." If we take the verb שׁוּף both times in the
signification of *insidiari, to lie in wait,* the expression ceases to be a promise of victory, although Dill-
mann thinks that even so the prophetic character
would remain, because the serpent is cursed, and the
conflict is arranged by God. But the expression
would then only assert that the consent of man to
the serpent,[1] which led to the fall of man, would be
changed into reciprocal, deadly hate. And even
grammatically this translation is inadmissible, for the
construction with the accusative of the person and
of the member demands a verb, which not only expresses an intended, but also an actual attack. Verbs
of hostile design are not construed in Hebrew with

[1] *Die Genesis,* Leipzig 1875, p. 89.

the double accusative, but only verbs of hostile meeting. Besides, there is no certain example of the use of שׁוּף in the signification of שָׁאַף; on the contrary, it is used in the Targum for דִּכָּא, טְחַן, and שְׁחַק. The Septuagint translates it both times τηρεῖν, to watch for; but Paul renders it in Rom. xvi. 20 by συντρίβειν, to bruise.

REMARK 3.—The point of the divine sentence is not directed against the seed of the serpent, but against the serpent, from whom the temptation went forth: "He will crush thee [not thy seed] on the head." Through however many generations the active enmity between the seed of the woman and the seed of the serpent may endure, the seed of the woman will attain the victory, and this victory is ultimately a victory over the original seducer, over the originator of evil which has entered humanity, over the "Old Serpent."

§ 8. *The Banishment from Paradise.*

Man has now entered into a condition which is the product of his own will. Adam, in the language of God (Gen. iii. 22), "is become as one of us," that is, he has become his own master (*sui juris*); like the deity and the heavenly spirits, he is now a being in whom freedom and necessity interpenetrate. But this completion of himself has not such a character that its eternal duration is desirable. The enjoyment of the tree of life would only tend to his destruction.

Hence man is driven from Paradise. Every evening sky directs his look to that which he has lost. Cherub and sword at the portals of Paradise warn him that the entrance to communion with God is forbidden him in his present condition, and will only be possible when he shall have become different. Henceforth the way to life passes through death (*per mortificationem et mortem*). The appearance of the cherub and the sword was terrible, but also comforting. God permitted Himself still to be seen, and even if it was in His anger, yet behind it was the expressed design of His love.

REMARK.—The Biblical conception considers the cherub as a real heavenly being, but the form which is given to it changes; it is symbolical and visionary. In the Babylonio-Assyrian mythology winged steers appear as the bearers of God's throne, and God in the form of a steer is called *alpu*, and also, as Lenormant has discovered, *kirubu*. The Babylonio-Assyrian verb *karâbu* signifies to be great or mighty; the adjective *karubu* is the synonym of *rubu*.[1] It is remarkable that in Ezekiel steer and cherub are interchanged (Ezek. x. 14). Everywhere the Biblical cherubs are bearers of the glory of God as He appears in the world, and here in the history of Paradise they are the warders of the access to Him.

[1] See Friedrich Delitzsch, *Lage des Paradieses*, Leipzig 1881, p. 154.

§ 9. *The Beginnings of the History outside of Paradise.*
(1) *Commencement of the Two Kinds of Seed in the Human Race.*

First after mankind, passing from their original condition of childhood, had attained maturity of moral character, the process of generation began; hence it is said (Gen. v. 3) that "Adam begat a son in his own likeness, after his own image." The potencies of sin and grace were both actualized in him. In this dualistic condition, whose wretchedness (Rom. vii. 24) was concealed by their faith, Adam and his wife became the first parents of the human race. The conflict between the good and evil in them secured at once through the first procreations a historical objectivity. As the evil arising from freedom of choice preceded the good arising from the same source, so the bad child preceded the good. The child which was expected to be a blessing became a curse. Cain could indeed have ruled over the sin which was lying in wait for him (Gen. iv. 2); but he did not do it, and thus fell into the hands of him who was a murderer from the beginning (John viii. 44; 1 John iii. 12). After grace has entered the human race contemporaneously with the utterance of the promise, all those who scornfully reject this grace like Cain isolate themselves from the seed of the woman, which carries the power of victory in itself, and become a seed of the serpent. The murder of Abel by Cain is the first bruise in the heel which the seed of the woman suffers from the seed of the serpent.

REMARK. — It is particularly the Gospel of John which discriminates between two kinds of men : those who are of God, and those who are not of God, but are of the evil one, or of the devil. In fact, there are many good and bad natural traits which are inherited, and which present the mental and ethical nature of men in an endlessly manifold commingling, yet this individual constitution has no decided moral value. Men, however differently the moral potencies in them are commingled, are all alike in this, that they are destitute of the righteousness which avails with God. Everything depends upon whether man gives himself to the power of grace or of evil, and so whether he stamps the innate good traits, or the innate evil traits, as the character of his personality.

§ 10. *The Beginnings of the History outside of Paradise.*
(2) *Commencement of Sacrifice.*

The narrative concerning the sacrifices of the brothers is instructive in the following particulars :—

(1) Sacrifice in its origin is not the satisfaction of a divine command, but of an inward need. We can even conclude, from the fact that Cain was the first one who offered sacrifice, that we have to do, not with the fulfilment of a divine command, but with a performance which proceeded from a more or less pure feeling of dependence.

(2) The sacrifice is in all its kinds a gift, an offering (מִנְחָה, δῶρον, γέρας, προσφορά). It is founded in the

consecration (*sacratio*), and is completed in the oblation (*oblatio*).

(3) It does not begin before man has left Paradise, and is the first step in the re-establishment of the original relation between man and God on the one side, and the natural world on the other, occupying with reference to both a mediatorial relation.

(4) The bloody offering contains the expiatory element, which is wanting in the vegetable offering, and therefore takes the precedence of it ; but

(5) Every offering is worthless without the right internal state of the one bringing it.   Abel offered by faith (Heb. xi. 4) animal sacrifices, which were types of the true vicarious sacrifice, and as he shed his own blood he was a type of the offering whose blood speaks better than that of Abel.

REMARK.—The history of Adam represents almost a thousand years.   Perhaps he is only the representative of this period, but the Biblical account really indicates such a great age.   Josephus appeals for it to an antique tradition outside the Bible (*Antiquities*, I. iii. 9).   In the one hundred and thirtieth year of his life Adam becomes the father of Seth.   Only a passing allusion is made to the daughters of Adam (Gen. v. 4).   Cain's wife was one of his sisters, for the marriage with sisters first became incest at a later period.   That which we read in Gen. iv. and v. are only fragments, of which the connecting links are wanting.   The tendency of Biblical historiography is ethical, is didactic.   The history is only the means, not the end. Hence from the tradition, which at the time of the original author flowed more richly, only *disjecta membra* are united together.

§ 11. *The Beginnings of the History outside of Paradise.* (3) *The Two Lines.*

From Cain and Seth, who took the place of Abel, the ancestral tree branches off into two lines, characterized by two phases of development, which, if man had not fallen, would have been only two sides of one development. Cain is the first builder of a city, and with Enos began the congregational character of divine service. The city Enoch, is the remote beginning of the world-empire, and Enos' congregation of Jehovah is the remote beginning of the church. In Lamech, the seventh in the Cainitic line, the direction towards that which is worldly rose to a Titanic defiance; and in Enoch, the seventh in the line of promise, the inward tendency is deepened to the point of a loving fellowship with God, which rendered him immortal. Even Enoch's son, although he finally died, lived longer than any of the Antediluvians. Enoch was taken away at a comparatively early age, for long life was even then not the highest good. The curse of sin made it one long woe; therefore Lamech hopes that in his son, the tenth in the line of promise, the period of the curse will have a comforting termination. This hope to a certain extent did not deceive him, for with Noah, after the judicial catastrophe, a new period began in which grace formed a barrier against the curse.

C

REMARK 1.—The two genealogical tables contain, besides Enoch and Lamech, different names, and pursue different ends. The Cainitic extends only to the seventh member, because in it the worldly, Cainitic development culminates; the Sethitic, however, leads from the primitive history to that of the flood. The heathen mythology stands in undeniable connection with the persons of the Cainitic genealogical table. A connection exists, although not an etymological one, between Jabal and Jubal, the two sons, and Apollo, between Tubal-Cain and Vulcan, Naamah and Venus, whose name, like that of Naamah, goes back to the Sanscrit *vanas*, delight, grace. Heathen mythology has deified partly natural objects, partly the men of the primitive history.

REMARK 2.—The names אָדָם, אִישׁ, and אֱנוֹשׁ, represent three stadia of the primitive history, namely, that of the primitive man, who is called אָדָם, as γη-γενής, *earth-born*; that of the husband of the wife (אִישׁ, equivalent to 'insh, which indicates *sociability, familiarity*); and that of man as subject to death (אֱנוֹשׁ, from אנשׁ, *to be sickly*, compare the Assyrian *ênšu*, weak). The Biblical Enoch corresponds to Gayômert of the Persian myth, whose name signifies mortal life.

§ 12. *The Termination of the History outside of Paradise, or the Judgment of the Flood.*

With the increase of the human race moral corruption increased. The distinction between the two lines disappeared. The boundaries drawn by the Creator between the world of men and spirits was broken through. The animal and demoniacal evil threatened to nullify the realization of the divine decree of mercy. Therefore, after a gracious respite of one hundred and twenty years had brought no improvement, God sent the flood, which destroyed man and the animals living in their neighbourhood. But this relapse of the earth into the stadium of the primitive waters (תְּהוֹם) was designed to effect a new beginning in the history of salvation. Noah, who remained true to God, was rescued, and became the deliverer of the human race, and of the animal world which was directly connected with it. In view of the judgment of the flood, the relation of God to man began to take on a deeper condescension by means of a covenant; and with Noah, the righteous man, began the typical mediatorial relations. The flood is a type of baptism (1 Pet. iii. 21), and the ark is a type of the church.

REMARK 1.—When the heathen mythology speaks of marriages between gods and men, and on the contrary, Gen. vi. 1–8, of marriages between the sons of the gods and the daughters of men, that view is most probable which understands the sons of God as prominent men resembling the gods. We are not to understand thereby demons, for only beings of the same species can have fruitful sexual intercourse, but demoniacal men who became the instruments of demons.

REMARK 2.—The hundred and twenty years are,

according to the Babylonio - Assyrian sexagesimal system, a double *sosse* (60 + 60), for *susu* is the Babylonian term for a sum of sixty.   Yet the one hundred and twenty years can also be explained according to the Biblical symbolism of numbers ; for forty is a number which indicates a period of waiting and transition, hence one hundred and twenty, the tripling of this number, indicates a crisis.

REMARK 3.—The Biblical narrative does not demand an absolutely universal deluge, for it measures its height by the top of one of the mountains of Ararat. The flood was in so far universal as it destroyed the entire human race then living. That was its only object.   But, on the other hand, the universality of the tradition of the flood which is to be found even among the nations of interior Africa (*e.g.* the Hereró), and of Northern India (*e.g.* the Kolhs), is a powerful proof of the historical unity of the human race.   The Babylonio-Assyrian account of the flood, which was made known in 1872, cannot be the original of the Biblical, for the tradition there appears to be transformed mythologically and locally.   The hero of the flood, Xisuthros,[1] is there caught up among the gods into the abode of the blessed ; hence he is confounded with Enoch.   And the mountain on which the ark landed is placed by this tradition in the neighbourhood of Babylon ; it is called *Nizir*, which is the name of the southern spur of the Armenian highlands.

---

[1] *Xi* is equivalent to the Sumerian *Zi*, which signifies life.

§ 13. *The Foundation of the Post-diluvian History, or the Covenant of the Rainbow.*

After Noah had left the ark, which had landed on a mountain of Ararat, with his family, he built an altar and sacrificed upon it burnt-offerings. Paradise, and the presence of God upon the threshold of Paradise, have now vanished from the earth. The suppliant hereafter looks upward; the one bringing a sacrifice raises therefore a place upon the earth. The offering is called עֹלָה, *that which ascends.* Earth and heaven are now separated. But God, receiving the sacrifice of thankful adoration with favour, promises that the progressive energy of the curse shall now be restrained through the predominating energy of grace. He renews the creative blessing, renders animals subject anew to man, allows the enjoyment of animal food, but with the exclusion of blood, and sanctions the capital punishment of him who lays hands on the life of his brother, created like him in the image of God. This Noachian covenant is until the present the gracious power which preserves the world, which assures the continuance of the human race; and the bow in the clouds is still the sign of the victory which grace won over wrath.

REMARK 1.—The threatening of death, with its reverse side, the promise of life, and in general the relation of God to those who were first created, does not yet fall under the conception of a covenant; hence Hos. vi. 7 is not to be translated, "*Like Adam* they have transgressed the covenant," but like men, that is, as sinful men are wont to do.   The God who threatens and promises remains exalted above man ; the God who makes a covenant goes down in condescension, and places Himself to a certain extent on the same level with him.   The covenant is an act through which God condescendingly assures what He promises, and this takes place first between God and Noah before and after the flood.

REMARK 2.—The Synagogue reckons seven Noachian commandments :—(1) The prohibition of idolatry; (2) of blasphemy; (3) of incest; (4) of murder; (5) of theft; (6) of the flesh of animals which are yet alive (*membrum de vivo*); (7) the institution of magisterial power.   Of these seven commands, Gen. ix. 1–7 contains only the fourth, sixth, and seventh.   The command, Gen. ix. 6, leaves the execution of punishment still undetermined; it lays it only in general in the hand of men, and demands it of him as the fulfilment of a duty, without allowing a ransom ($\pi o\iota\nu\acute{\eta}$), as in the Homeric poems.

§ 14. *The Internal and External Separation of the Peoples.*

It is soon apparent that the internal root of corruption has not been destroyed.   When Noah after his drunkenness had clarified his spirit through the pain of repentance, he looks through that which his sons have done into the future of mankind, which is ethnographically and ethically distinguished in a threefold way. After the foundation of the difference between the nations has thus been laid in the house of Noah, it is still further carried out in Shinar (*Sumir*), that is, in the land on the lower Euphrates. The process of separation in language which God introduces to check the selfish and unspiritual effort of mankind for unity, is the beginning of the nationalities. With these nationalities arose at the same time the heathen, with their different languages and religions. If there is still in this chaos a ray of light, it is necessary for the benefit of mankind that means should be found for its preservation. That this should take place within the line of Shem, appears from the programme delineated by Noah while under the influence of the Spirit. Shem is, from this time on, the centre-point of the history of salvation. The line of the covenant goes through Shem.

REMARK 1.—The breaking up of the united human race into peoples with different languages was a divine act for the good of man; for by this means a barrier was made against sin, which, without this separating wall of the language, would have attained a terrible intensity. Now, however, the immoral and irreligious products of one nation are not equally destructive to another; and many false religions are better than one, since they paralyze one another. Even war, which arises from the selfish character of nationalities, is better than the idle peace of universal estrangement from God, for the demon of war arouses the peoples and drives them to God.

REMARK 2.—Babel signified originally *bab ilu, gate of God ;* in Sumerian *ka dingira,* which has the same meaning. The Biblical narrative understands the name ominously as an emblem of the confusion of tongues which took place.

SECOND PERIOD.

FROM THE ELECTION OF ABRAM UNTIL THE EMIGRATION
OF THE FAMILY OF JACOB INTO EGYPT. THE PERIOD
OF THE AGE OF THE PATRIARCHS, OR OF THE SEPARA-
TION AMONG THE NATIONS.

§ 15. *The New Beginning and the Remnant of the Old.*

THE leading of Abram out from the heathen world
may be compared to the separation between the
earthly and heavenly waters on the second day of
creation. Since the strife between good and evil has
entered into the world, a new separation of that which
is dissimilar is always the signal of all true progress.
Abram's native house lay within the kingdom of
Nimrod. Whether at that time the non-Semitic
(Kushitish) or the Semitic population was dominant
we do not know, but it is certain that both had fallen
into polytheism. Because the Shemites had forsaken
the God of Shem,[1] the blessing of Noah could not be
realized in them. God therefore made the point of
light, which had not grown dim in Abram, the tenth

[1] Josh. xxiv. 2 : "And Joshua said to all the people, Thus saith
Jehovah, God of Israel, Your fathers dwelt on the other side of the
river from old time, Terah the father of Abraham and the father of
Nahor, and they served other gods."

41

from Shem, to the starting-point of a new development.
Abram, "the one," [1] became the holy root of the good
olive tree of Israel. But the national form into which
the salvation now enters is only a means to its end.
Melchizedek in doing homage to Abram recognises in
him God's chosen instrument, and Abram in subordi-
nating himself to the Hamitic priestly king, whose
knowledge of God dates from beyond the separation
of mankind into nations, bows himself as the new
beginning before the remnant of the old. The priestly
stem of Israel bows beforehand in the presence of an
appearance outside the law, and it appears, by way of
prelude, that the law will find its accomplishment in
an end which resembles the beginning, whose remnant
is Melchizedek.

REMARK 1.—In Melchizedek's thanking Abram and
blessing him, we have the consciousness of the nations
typically portrayed, that they are indebted to the
people of Abram for the mediation of salvation ; and
in the subordination of Abram to Melchizedek the
consciousness of Israel is typically portrayed, that it
is only a chosen instrument for the salvation of the
nations, and that after it has fulfilled its calling it is
destined to disappear with its nationality in the
redeemed human race.

REMARK 2.—The determination of Terah to emigrate

---

[1] Mal. ii. 15 : "And did he not make one? Yet he had the residue
of the Spirit. And wherefore the one? *Because* he was seeking the
seed of God," etc. Compare Isa. li. 2 : "Look unto Abraham your
father, and unto Sarah that bare you : for I called him alone," etc. ;
Ezek. xxxiii. 24.

to Canaan, which existed before the call of Abram, was doubtless connected with the movement of the Babylonian Shemites from south to north, of which Gen. xii. forms the beginning, and whose continuation is the emigration of the Canaanites (compare Gen. x. 6). The narrative here, however, manifests no interest in the history of the peoples as such, but only as it has a bearing on the history of redemption, and this interest fastens on single individuals.

§ 16. *The Ethical Character of the New Beginning.*

The call of Abram had in view a family of God, and in this family a people of God, and in this people the God-man. The ethical character of the new beginning is determined by this.

(1) It is a work of *grace* which is prepared, hence everything proceeds in the history of the patriarchs contrary to nature. The divine name which is peculiar to the patriarchal history is God Almighty. Grace always raises itself on the foundation of the natural after it has first destroyed it; thus the body of Abram must become as "good as dead" (Rom. iv. 19; Heb. xi. 12) before he could become the father of the son of promise.

(2) It is a work of the *future* which is prepared. The present stands in sharp contrast with this future. The whole life of the patriarchs therefore flows on in hope and against hope. The true domain of their lives is in the time of redemption, to which the divine name Jehovah is peculiar.

(3) It is a work of the *world to come* which is prepared; a work proceeding from that world, and tending towards it. Hence the divine leading of the patriarchs tends to disgust them not only with the present, but in general with temporal things. They died weary of life, and sought, as is said in Heb. xi. 16, after a better fatherland.

(4) It is God's *own work* which is prepared, not man's work. That which God demands before all things else of the patriarchs is a state of mind which is receptive for this work of God, which inquires after it, and blends with it; in a word, *faith.* Abraham believed (Gen. xv. 6), and thus became the father of the congregation of faith.[1] His faith became his righteousness before he received and obeyed the command of circumcision. The period of the patriarchs is the period of faith before the intermediate coming in of the law, and hence it is the Old Testament type of the New Testament period of faith after the doing away of the law. To this evangelical character, which is peculiar to the time of the patriarchs, correspond also the modes of God's revelation.

REMARK 1.—When God says (Ex. vi. 3) that He appeared to the patriarchs as God Almighty (*El Shaddai*), and was not made known to them by His name Jehovah, the meaning is that they experienced divine acts, which in the midst of the contradictory

---

[1] Rom. iv. 16 : "For this cause *it is* of faith, that *it may be* according to grace ; to the end that the promise may be sure to all the seed ; not to that only which is of the law, but to that also which is of the faith of Abraham, who is the father of us all."

present ensured the fulfilment of the promise, but that this fulfilment remained for them at a remote distance.

REMARK 2.—With regard to the significance of the mention of faith in connection with the Old Testament history, see Michael Baumgarten on Gen. xv. 6, *Theologischer Commentar zum Pentateuch*, Kiel 1843-1844.

§ 17. *The Divine Modes of Revelation.*

God spoke to the patriarchs in the depth of their spirits, but He revealed Himself also in manifold other ways ; in dreams, in ecstatic sleep (תַּרְדֵּמָה), in prophetic beholding while they were awake, or it is simply said that He appeared to them (Gen. xv. 17). That, however, which is new and characteristic of the period of the patriarchs is the manner of revelation which is mediated through angels. What Jacob saw in the dream of the ladder reaching to heaven is from that time on the characteristic of the history of redemption, and occurs in the time of the patriarchs more frequently than elsewhere, according to the law of redemptive history that there is a predominant intensity in every beginning. The appearances of the angel of Jehovah or of God form the culminating point of all these *angelophanies*, which first enter after the conclusion of the covenant (Gen. xv.), and whose object and end are to be judged by this commencement (*terminus a quo*). On the one hand this angel is even called Jehovah and God,[1] and he

---

[1] Ex. iii. 4: "And when Jehovah [compare ver. 2: the angel of Jehovah] saw that he turned aside to see, God called unto him," etc.

calls himself God ;[1] on the other hand, he cannot be the sender himself, but the sent (לְאָךְ is equivalent to שָׁלַח, Gen. xxiv. 7 ; Num. xx. 16). He is, as the prophecy in Zechariah[2] and the New Testament regard him, a real angel,[3] yet one of a thousand through whom God chose to reveal Himself personally, as later in the man Jesus, hence in a manner prefiguring and preparing His incarnation, which was the end of the covenant. And since the angel appeared in human form, this mode of revelation was especially familiar and evangelical.

REMARK.—Even just after the fall of man a theophany is related (Gen. iii. 8 sq.); but the narrative purposely avoids the expression which commonly occurs in the later theophanies, " and he appeared," which we first meet in Gen. xii. 7. It should here be observed : (1) That it is only related of the patriarchs, but not of any of their contemporaries, that God appeared to them. (2) Such divine appearances are narrated— (a) without any closer indication of the time and condition, Gen. xii. 7, xxvi. 2, xxxv. 9 ; (b) with an indication of time, " by night," Gen. xxvi. 24 ; (c) with an indication of the condition, " in a vision," Gen. xv. 1, compare Num. xxiv. 4, 16, that is, in a condi-

---

[1] Gen. xxxi. 11, 13 : " And the angel of God spake unto me. . . . I am the God of Bethel ;" Ex. iii. 6 : " And he [ver. 2 : the angel of Jehovah] said, I am the God of thy father," etc.

[2] Zech. iii. 2 : " And Jehovah [compare ver. 2 : the angel of Jehovah] said unto Satan, Jehovah rebuke thee," etc.

[3] Jude, ver. 9 : " But Michael the archangel, when, contending with the devil, he disputed about the body of Moses, durst not bring against him a railing judgment, but said, The Lord rebuke thee."

tion of prophetic beholding; or (*d*) in "a dream," compare Gen. xxviii. 10 sq. with Gen. xlviii. 3. This is the only case where God appears to a patriarch in a dream. Otherwise the dream is the medium through which the future appears in images, Gen. xxxi. 10 (to Jacob); Gen. xxxvii. (to Joseph); especially to the heathen, Gen. xl. xli. (to Pharaoh and the prisoners); and where it is said that God revealed Himself to them in a dream, the narrative does not state that He appeared to them, but that He came to them, Gen. xx. 3 (to Abimelech), xxxi. 24 (to Laban); that is, that He caused them to feel His nearness overpoweringly.

§ 18. *The Promises.*

As this revelation of Jehovah in His angel was determined by the form of the New Testament future which was to be prefigured, so the words of the promise concerning the future, which was to be prefigured, were determined by the form of the present. Unity based on consanguinity, community ordered by law, and the firm possession of a country, are the three things which make a multitude of mankind into a people and a state. Hence the promises to the patriarchs have their primary reference to the future possession of the land in which they are pilgrims, to the propagation of their race, and to kings.[1] Abraham

---

[1] Gen. xvii. 6 : "And I will make thee exceeding fruitful, and I will make nations of thee, and kings shall come out of thee;" and Gen. xxxv. 11.

is to be the ancestor of a people of God, an ancestor
of many peoples connected with them by blood; but
the promise of the blessing of the nations in the seed
of the patriarchs, which is given thrice to him, and
once each to Isaac and Jacob, gives him even for the
wider circles of the non-Abrahamic nations a central
significance.   The nations' desire for a blessing will
turn to Abraham and his seed, and so the fulness of
blessing which he possesses will become a source of
blessing to the nations.   Paul appends (Gal. iii. 16)
to this expression " in thy seed " the explanatory expression of the history of fulfilment, " which is Christ."
Even the author of the Messianic Psalm (lxxii. 17)
proceeds from the same presupposition.   He who is
the personal end of the " seed of the woman," that is,
of the human race, is for the apostle as well as the
psalmist the personal end of the seed of Abraham,
that is, of the people of Israel.   And with reason, for
the history of redemption progresses gradually, but in
every element of its progress that which it will ultimately bring to light is already contained as in process
of becoming.

§ 19. *The Prophecy.*

Abraham is indeed called a prophet (Gen. xx. 7;
Ps. cv. 15), yet we nowhere read of divine revelations
through him to others.   But we have benedictions
of Isaac and Jacob, which consist in the appropriate
announcement and application of future things propheti-
cally seen.   The blessing of the first-born (Gen. xxvii.),

which Jacob obtains through artifice, bestows on him
Canaan, renders the more remote as well as the con-
sanguineous nations subject to him, and conditions the
blessing and curse of men by the relation which they
hold to the one who has been blessed. The benediction which Esau subsequently receives is only the
shadow of a blessing, but a shadow which dimmed
the history of Israel until the time of the final
catastrophe of Jerusalem. The blessing of the
first - born which Jacob then bestowed upon Judah
(Gen. xlix.) is none other than the one received from
Isaac.

Descending from the three (Reuben, Simeon, Levi)
who in age were next entitled to it, he makes him
the prince (נָגִיד), while the birthright (בְּכוֹרָה), that is,
the twofold inheritance, falls to the double tribe of
Joseph, the saviour of the house of Israel (1 Chron. v.
1). The turning-point from tribal dominion to the
dominion of the world is marked by the coming to
Shiloh [1] (Gen. xlix. 10; compare 1 Sam. iv. 12, 1
Kings xiv. 4).

This is the return of Judah to his people after
victorious conflict, for which Moses in his benediction
prays in behalf of the tribe (Deut. xxxiii. 7). Judah
until this coming to Shiloh was the leader of the
tribes, and continued to be so even until the beginning
of the time of the Judges. But the real fulfilment of
this benediction became this, that the kingdom of the
promise was transferred to Judah, and that he was the

[1] See Delitzsch's *Messianic Prophecies*, Edin. 1880, p. 34 sq.

chosen royal tribe of Israel, out of which the first and
the second David went forth.[1]

§ 20. *The Triad of Patriarchs and the Types.*

Three is the number of a completed process. The
third member is the sum of both the others, and as
the end is stronger than the beginning, so, as a rule,
the middle is weaker than the beginning and end
($-\smile \acute{}$). Thus the history of the patriarchs moves to
its goal. Isaac's character is as passive as his name,
which does not express his own, but Abraham's act.
In almost all that is related of him, Abraham's history
repeats itself. On the contrary, Abraham's history is
a new, high, energetic beginning. His life, in spite of
many eclipses, is a progress from faith to faith; and
Jacob's history, in spite of many shadows, is wonder-
fully guided by God's loving-kindness and truth. His
life makes the total impression, that salvation is "not
of works" (Rom. ix. 11), and it attains in Peniel as
high a point as Abraham's on Moriah. Not the blessing of the first-born secured from Esau by cunning,
but that obtained from God by wrestling, becomes the
basis of the nation which bears the name Israel, born
of the labour of prayer and repentant tears (Hos.
xii. 5).

In its climaxes, the history of the patriarchs takes

---

[1] Heb. vii. 14, first clause : "For it is evident that our Lord hath
sprung out of Judah." Rev. v. 5 : " Behold, the Lion of the tribe of
Judah," etc.

on a typical form. The type, however, hastens on before the prophecy. At the end of the history of the patriarchs, prophecy designated the tribe of Judah as the starting-place of the future Christ. But the ground-tone of his image is only of a royal character. The transaction on Mount Moriah, however, is a type incorporated by God into the history, a type of the sacrifice of the only begotten Son, which the Father will at length bring for the human race, and at the same time of the self-sacrifice of the Son, who goes willingly to death. Also, the struggle at Jabbok is typical. Peniel and Moriah stand related to each other like Gethsemane and Golgotha.

REMARK 1.—Instead of the names Abram and Sarai, the narrator, after the epoch indicated in Gen. xvii. 5, 15, uses without exception the names Abraham and Sarah—similarly as in Acts the name Saul after xiii. 9 disappears. On the contrary, the name of Jacob, in spite of the change into Israel, is retained, and the name Israel is used only as a variation for it. For the names Abraham and Sarah indicate a new position, by which the former become antiquated. On the other hand, the name Israel indicates a spiritual conduct, determined by faith, beside which the natural conduct, determined by flesh and blood, still continues. The patriarch who bore the names Jacob and Israel is therein a prototype of the people which sprung from him.

REMARK 2.—The type is, on the one hand, the work of God, the framer of history; on the other, it is the self-announcement of the coming One, like the shadow

which accompanies the Christ throughout the Old
Testament in His process of coming. The type is
prophecy in deed (*vaticinium reale*), and is distinguished from prophecy in word (*vaticinium verbale*)
by this, that it takes place outside of the sphere of
human consciousness and human freedom, and that it
is only recognised through the medium of God's word,
which explains it, or by looking back from the standpoint of the goal upon the preceding history.

§ 21. *The Covenant and its Sign.*

The next tendency of the redemptive history in
this second period, toward effecting a separation in
the mass of the nations, finds expression in the
covenant with Abraham (Gen. xv.) and in the sign
of that covenant. The covenant with Noah concerned
the human race, which was still undivided, and had
respect to the most universal presuppositions in the
realization of salvation, namely the foundations of the
natural and social life. But the call of Abraham has
its goal in a redemptive people, and also the covenant
with Abraham concerns only mediately mankind; it
has first to do with Israel. Abraham perceives (Gen.
xv.) that the course of his posterity to the promised
elevation goes through deep humiliation. One act
of deliverance places his seed in possession of that
which has been promised, namely the deliverance
from the land of bondage. And the sign of the
covenant of circumcision is designed to assure Abraham,

and all who belong to his family or enter it, that although they are impure by nature, yet that their nature is sanctified, and that they are to be the origin of a people with a sanctified nature. As God by means of the firmament divided between the waters above and beneath, so He now divided between the redemptive people and the peoples of the world, until the time when the heavenly water of baptism takes the place of circumcision, which breaks through this national wall of partition, and not only sanctifies the nature, but also through regeneration lays the foundation for a radical change in it.

REMARK.—The Old Testament religion begins with the sanctification of the natural life, and makes this a tutorial means (Gal. iii. 24), which tends to sanctification of the personal life. The New Testament religion, on the contrary, begins with the sanctification of the personal life, creating in the centre of man the principle of a new life, whose object is to bring also the natural life under his sway. It belongs to the peripheral character of the Old Testament religion, that it takes common, human, heathen customs into its service, and re-stamps them, as even circumcision, which is a divine ordinance, connected with a usage already existing; for the old civilised nations, especially the Egyptians, as also yet many negro and Indian tribes, regarded the removal of the foreskin as necessary to purity of body.

THIRD PERIOD.

FROM THE SOJOURN IN EGYPT UNTIL THE ARRIVAL IN
SHILOH. THE PERIOD OF THE DEVELOPMENT OF
ISRAEL, AND THE SPRING-TIME IN THE LAND OF
PROMISE.

§ 22. *The Development of the Patriarchal Family into a Nation.*

THE pilgrim life of the patriarchs gradually came to
a stand-still, hence the danger of intermarriages
with the Canaanites arose. Under these circumstances
the providential leading of Joseph became the means of
hindering their settlement in a manner contrary to
the promise, and of preparing a suitable place in
Egypt for the independent ripening of the family of
Jacob to a nation. It was an arrangement of the
divine wisdom that the family of Jacob were sunk in
the currents of the national life of Egypt,—which as
scarcely any other was regulated by law, penetrated
by religion, and thoroughly cultivated in the most
manifold way,—in order to go forth after four hundred
and thirty years (Ex. xii. 40), or two hundred and
fifteen years (according to the Septuagint rendering [1]

---

[1] The rendering is as follows: ἡ δὲ κατοίκησις τῶν υἱῶν Ἰσραὴλ ἣν
κατῴκησαν ἐν γῇ Αἰγύπτῳ καὶ ἐν γῇ Χαναὰν ἔτη τετρακόσια τριάκοντα.
" Now the sojourning of the children of Israel which they spent

of the same passage, compare Gal. iii. 17), as a nation,
which was the spiritual antitype of this heathen,
natural type. From a few people in Egypt arose a
great nation (Deut. xxvi. 5), but one which became
more and more estranged from the God of redemptive
history (Ezek. xxiii. 8, 19, 27). During the period
of the Egyptian sojourn, falls the reign of the Hyksôs
(Shepherd kings), which lasted several hundred years.
These kings were Semitic usurpers, who combined the
Egyptian worship of Ra with the Canaanitic worship
of Set or Sutech, who is almost the same as Baal
and especially Molech (Amos v. 26). After they had
been driven out by Amosis (Ahmes), one of the kings
of the eighteenth dynasty, that new king (Ex. i. 8)
arose under whom the oppression of Israel began. The
new king is a representative of the native dynasty,
which after the expulsion of the Hyksôs came to
power, and no longer remembered what Joseph had
done for the land, and especially for the royal house.
Simultaneously with the oppression of Israel began,
under the restored native royal power, the reanimation of the national consciousness in the better part
of God's people. The Israelitish proper names in
Exodus vi., Numbers i., and in the first chapters of
Chronicles, present a vivid picture of the state of
feeling at that time. The names of the father and

in the land of Egypt and of Canaan was four hundred and thirty
years." Not only Hellenistic tradition, but also Palestinian, testifies
that the sojourn of the Israelites in Egypt lasted two hundred and
fifteen (210) years. See the *Pesikta* of Rab Kahana, edited by Solomon
Buber, Lyck 1868, fol. 47ᵇ.

mother of Moses, Amram and Jochebed, contain the two great thoughts which filled and animated his soul. The name Amram signifies *the people is high*, and thus indicates that Israel is an exalted people; and the name Jochebed signifies that *Jehovah is glory*, and affirms that Jehovah is exalted above the gods of the heathen, and hence of Egypt.

REMARK.—The Israelites were compelled to build for Pharaoh the magazine cities Pithom and Ramses. The name Ramses indicates a Pharaoh of this name, and not Ramses I., who reigned only one full year, but Ramses II. Miamun (the beloved of Amun), during whose reign, according to two papyrus rolls in Leyden, *Apuriu*, which without doubt are the same as *Ibrim* (Hebrews), are mentioned as compulsory labourers in the building of a *Bechennu*, one of the fortified magazines. According to this, the oppression of Israel fell in the sixty-six years of the reign of this second Ramses. The first four kings of the nineteenth dynasty are Ramses I., 1443 B.C.; Sethos I. (*Seti*) 1439; Ramses II., 1388; and Menephthes (*Merneph-tah*), 1322. The year of the Exodus is, as Lepsius, Ebers, and most now think, the year 1314 B.C.

§ 23. *The Exodus.*

The opinion which even Schiller adopted in his *Sendung Moses*[1] may now be considered as established.

---

[1] This article first appeared in the tenth number of the *Thalia*, 1790; see Delitzsch's *Pentateuch-kritische Studien;* first article on the *Lepers-Tora*, in Luthardt's *Zeitschrift*, Leipzig 1880, pp. 1–10.

The expulsion of the lepers under Amenophis, or Menephthes, is the event to which the Egyptian myth has distorted the exodus of Israel from Egypt.[1] Ramses II. Miamun is the Pharaoh of the oppression, and his son, Mernephtah (the beloved of Ptah), is the Pharaoh of the exodus. The princess who rescued Moses in Tanis was probably a daughter of Seti, and a sister of Ramses II.[2] The foundling was brought up by Pharaoh's daughter like a prince;[3] but when he was grown up, he regarded "the reproach of Christ greater riches than the treasures of Egypt" (Heb. xi. 24–27). Although the name Moses may be identical with the Egyptian *mes* (*mesu*), which signifies child, yet, understood as a Hebrew word, it is a hint at the history of him who, drawn out of the waters of the Nile, drew his people out of the waters of Egypt.[4] In the solitude of Arabia he matured for this high calling.

The theophany in the burning thorn-bush assured him that he and his people were now to get a sight of the fire of the divine wrath without being consumed thereby. Plague after plague comes upon Egypt, which disappoints Israel's hope again and again. But in this fiery furnace of affliction (Deut. iv. 20; com-

---

[1] Josephus, *Contra Apionem*, i. 26 sq.

[2] Compare Ebers, *Durch Gosen nach Sinai*, Leipzig 1872, p. 82 sq.

[3] Acts vii. 21, 22 : "And when he was cast out, Pharaoh's daughter took him up, and nourished him for her own son. And Moses was instructed in all the wisdom of the Egyptians," etc.

[4] Isa. lxiii. 11, first clause : "Then he remembered the days of old, Moses, and his people. Where is he that brought them up out of the sea with the shepherd of his flock ?"

pare Isa. xlviii. 10) the silver gleam of the name
Jehovah shines for Israel. God has now formed a
people as His peculiar possession, and is now called
Jehovah, as the God of free grace ruling in this people.
As on the third day of creation the continent, as the
birth-place of mankind, goes forth from the waters, so
in this third period Israel, as the birth-place of the
future God-man, goes forth from Egypt. The people
really come out of the waters,[1] marching through the
Red Sea, since God's miraculous interference lengthened
and heightened the time of the ebb-tide, out of just
those waters which, flowing back, buried the Egyptians ;
an event which is celebrated in the Scriptures as the
felling of *rahab*, that is, of the monster of the waters,
and as the piercing of the *tannin*, that is, of the dragon.[2]
This passage through the sea was, according to 1 Cor. x.
1 sq., Israel's baptism, namely, into Jehovah, and into
Moses his servant (Ex. xiv. 31).

REMARK 1.—The name Jehovah (יהוה) was not first
coined in the Mosaic period, but it received a particular specialization of its meaning. In itself considered,
the name Jehovah indicates the One whose nature
consists in being, which continually manifests itself
as existence, the One existing by and through Himself,
the eternal, and at the same time the eternally living
One. But at the time of Moses the name received,

---

[1] Isa. li. 10 : " Art thou not it which hath dried the sea, the waters
of the great deep ; that hath made the depths of the sea a way for the
ransomed to pass over ?" and Ps. civ. 7.

[2] Isa. li. 9, last clause : " Art thou not it that was cutting *rahab*,
and piercing the *tannin* ?"

through the explanation in Ex. iii. 14 sq., "I shall be what I shall be," a special direction towards the future. The name signifies from henceforth the One existing in the unlimited future, and in His being determining Himself with absolute freedom; hence the One who, without extraneous compulsion, so reveals Himself as His decree requires; in brief, the God of redemptive history, whose government has as its signature mercy and truth.

REMARK 2.—Those are everywhere important and significant turning-points in the history of redemption where the Old Testament Scriptures speak of faith:

(1) The beginning of the anterior history of the people of God;[1]

(2) The beginning of the period of the kingdom of God;[2]

(3) The beginning of the period when the kingdom of God was transferred to the heathen.[3]

§ 24. *The Egyptian Passover and the Beginning of the Kingdom of God.*

The leading of Israel out of Egypt is the Old Testament redemption. As the last of the ten plagues,

---

[1] Gen. xv. 6: "And he believed in Jehovah, and He counted it to him as righteousness."

[2] Ex. xiv. 31: "And Israel saw the mighty act which Jehovah performed upon the Egyptians; and the people feared Jehovah, and believed in Jehovah, and in Moses His servant."

[3] Jonah iii. 5: "And the men of Nineveh believed in God, and proclaimed a fast, and put on sackcloth, from the greatest of them even unto the least of them."

the destruction of the firstborn, visited Egypt, and
Israel received the command to sprinkle its doors with
the blood of the passover-lamb, it was not the blood of
the animal which changed the divine wrath into mercy
which spared[1] their firstborn, but the antitypical
redemption stood behind it, as yet a dumb, unrevealed
secret, for all the types spring from the invisible root
of their antitype. Even the song of Moses (Ex. xv.)
after Israel had crossed the Red Sea is typical; it is
the eternally significant counterpart of the song of the
Lamb (Rev. xv. 3).   It closes with the words, "Jehovah shall reign as king, for ever and ever."   A king
needs, in order really to be a king, a people ; such a
people Jehovah now has for the first time in Israel.[2]
The theocratic activity of God now begins, but the
national form of God's kingdom is merely its foundation.   Israel is only the firstborn of the nations.[3]

REMARK 1.—The Egyptian passover was a sacrifice,
for although an altar was wanting, it was nevertheless
stamped as a sacrifice :

(1) Through the separation of the lamb for the
purpose of a divine service ;

(2) Through the application of the blood with the
stalk of hyssop.

(3) Through the following religious meal.   It has,
with reference to the meal, the character of the peace-

---

[1] The word פֶּסַח signifies to *pass over, to spare*, compare Isa. xxxi. 5.

[2] Deut. xxxiii. 5 : "And He was king in Jeshurun," etc.

[3] Ex. iv. 22 : "And thou shalt say unto Pharaoh, Thus saith
Jehovah, My son, my firstborn is Israel."

offerings; the blood, as in all animal sacrifices, aimed at a mediatorial expiation. An innocent life is presented to God, behind which Israel seeks covering for its own life, burdened with guilt. The blood was sprinkled upon the doorposts, and especially upon the upper moulding; in the subsequent observances of the passover, it was poured out at the foot of the altar, and the pieces of fat were laid upon the fire of the altar (Ex. xxiii. 18, xxxiv. 25).

REMARK 2.—The name theocracy (θεοκρατία) was invented by Josephus.[1] When properly applied, it does not indicate a form of government, but a relation entered into between Jehovah and Israel, which does not demand any particular form of government, and is not excluded by any. The monarchy corresponds most to the theocracy, in so far as the theocratic relation will finally be completed in a *christocratic*.

§ 25. *Characteristics of the Legislation.*

As the people in the third month of the exodus were in the wilderness, they learned through Moses the high destiny intended for them, and answered the words of Jehovah with the promise, "All that Jehovah hath spoken we will do" (Ex. xix. 1–8, compare xxiv. 3, 7 sq.). After this unanimous and decisive answer began the giving of the law on Sinai, which forms the medium between its prelude in Marah[2] and its con-

---

[1] *Contra Apionem*, ii. 16.
[2] Ex. xv. 25, second clause: "There he made for them a statute and an ordinance" (compare Josh. xxiv. 25).

clusion in the plains of Moab. From its course and contents the following main aspects are derived :—

(1) It is a people to which the revelation from Sinai is directed. This revelation enters into the barriers of a nationality, and it cannot do this without accommodating itself to all that is incongruous in the character of the people to the idea of humanity.

(2) It is a people of which Aaron says, in order to excuse himself, that "they are bent on mischief" (Ex. xxxii. 22). Therefore the law must bind this people with a thousand bonds, in order to restrain its sinful inclination, and it must surround its demands with dreadful threatenings in order to secure itself.

(3) The law curses all those who do not absolutely fulfil all its commands,[1] and therefore leaves man only the threefold possibility, either carnally to ignore it, or to despair, or to take refuge in mercy.

(4) The law meets this flight for mercy with gracious promises, and gracious institutions. But these gracious institutions subserve the end in view only as shadows, and externally and temporally, as the Epistle to the Hebrews shows ; and to prevent that mercy from being sought wantonly, every step in this direction is defined with painful exactness ; and even the gospel elements in the law have a legal character. This character of the law corresponds to its mode of revela-

---

[1] Deut. xxvii. 26 : "Cursed be he who shall not establish the words of this law to do them," etc.

tion. It is not immediately the direct revelation of the one God, but is mediated through angels and men.[1]

§ 26. *The Essential Homogeneity of the Law in all the Phases of its Development.*

The characteristic features which have been indicated are peculiar to the law in all the stages of its development.   Deuteronomy is not distinguished therein from the Middle Books of the Pentateuch, and even Ezekiel's Tora of the future has the same physiognomy.   The description of the religion of the law is therefore independent of the results of Pentateuch criticism.   All parts of the Pentateuch recognise the wonderful acts of God by which the exodus of Israel from Egypt under Moses' leadership [2] was accompanied; [3] all presuppose that the Tora which gave Israel its stamp as the people of God flowed from a majestic revelation of God upon Mount Sinai.[4]

[1] Gal. iii. 20 : " Now a mediator is not a mediator of one ; but God is one."   Compare Deut. xxxiii. 2 : " Jehovah came from Sinai, and rose from Seir unto them ; He shined from Mount Paran, and He came with ten thousand saints ; from His right was a fiery law for them ;" Acts vii. 53 : "Ye who received the law as it was ordained by angels," etc.

[2] Hos. xii. 13 : "And by a prophet Jehovah brought Israel out of Egypt, and by a prophet was he preserved."   Isa. liii. 11 : "Then he remembered the days of old, Moses, and his people, saying, Where is he that brought them up out of the sea with the shepherd of his flock ?"

[3] Micah vii. 15 : "According to the day of thy coming out of the land of Egypt will I show thee marvellous things."

[4] Judg. v. 4, 5 : "Jehovah, when thou wentest out of Seir, when thou marchedst out of the field of Edom, the earth trembled, the

The Tora, in all its forms and codifications, consists of the demands of divine holiness, and of means provided for purification and atonement, and is everywhere the rule of life for a people which is not able to withdraw from externality and particularism, with which a nationality and a state are infected. It accommodates itself to deeply-rooted institutions and customs, such as the avenging of blood, slavery, polygamy, and marriage with a brother's wife, since it contents itself with an ameliorating, restricting, and regulating interference, and leaves here and there even important deficiencies, as, for example, in the reasons for divorce,[1] since it confines itself to that which can be attained in the present stage of the people's moral condition. In contrast with other ancient legislations, the Tora justifies its divine origin; but it is not less than all other legislations of the peoples, human, national, adapted to the age, and even on this account a standpoint which has been passed by for the new world which has been formed by Christianity.

REMARK.—Nowhere in the Tora is the non-Israelite, or the man as such, called the neighbour of the Israelite. Although in Lev. xix. 18, second clause, we read, "Thou shalt love thy neighbour as thyself;" yet in the parallel member, ver. 18, first clause, we

heavens also dropped, also the clouds dropped water; the mountains melted from before Jehovah, even this Sinai from before Jehovah God of Israel."

[1] Deut. xxiv. 1. Matt. xix. 8 : "He saith unto them, Moses, for your hardness of heart, suffered you to put away your wives: but from the beginning it hath not been so."

have these words: "Thou shalt not avenge, nor bear
a grudge against the children of thy people." The
legal regulations respecting the taking of usury (Deut.
xxiii. 20 sq.), and the non-exaction of debts in the
year of release (Deut. xv. 1–3), allowed the Israelites
to pursue a course with the stranger which was
forbidden with regard to a brother of the same nation.
The Israelite was not allowed to eat of any carcase,
but he might give it to the stranger (גֵּר), and also sell
it to the alien (נָכְרִי).[1] Deuteronomy is as exclusive as
all the rest of the legislation, nay, even more exclusive.
It modifies the law which pronounces the sentence of
death upon one pursuing the slave trade,[2] by limiting
it to the stealing and selling of an Israelite as a slave.

§ 27. *The Sacrificial Tora.*

The sacrificial worship was neither the first nor the
chief thing in the legislation.[3] It had previously
existed as traditional usage; and when the legislation
purified and regulated it, this was only a concession[4]
which was made to the human need of sacrifice, but

[1] Deut. xiv. 21: "Ye shall not eat any carcase: to the stranger that
is in thy gates thou mayest give it, or thou mayest sell it to the
alien," etc.

[2] Ex. xxi. 16 : "And he that stealeth a man or selleth him, if he
be found in his hand, shall surely be put to death."

[3] Jer. vii. 22: "For I did not speak with your fathers, nor
command them in the day that I brought them out of the land of
Egypt, concerning burnt-offering and sacrifice."

[4] Such a concession is indicated in Lev. xvii. 11 : "*I have given it
to you* [that is, the blood] upon the altar, to make an atonement for
your souls."

not without the dangers connected with it being foreseen. The greatest danger lay in the delusion, into which the people were likely to fall, that the gift as such was a sufficient compensation for the sin, — a delusion which the prophets oppose in such cutting expressions as Micah vi. 6–8. The sacrificial Tora itself therefore holds the elements of the atonement and of the offering wide apart. All which is consumed in fire upon the altar is not in itself of an atoning character, but is only acceptable to God on the presupposition that it is the offering of one who has been previously reconciled. The promise of reconciliation is absolutely connected with the blood alone, or with the offering on account of the blood. Hence the emptying of the blood from the sacrificial bowl, or the pressing out of the blood at the side of the altar, always precedes the offering itself; for a preliminary condition of every offering which is pleasing to God, is the atonement mediated through the life-blood of the guiltless animal which is devoted to death. But between the person of the man and the animal, which mediates through its blood, there is an endless difference. And, moreover, the sacrificial animal suffers an involuntary death, contrary to its will, while the atoning character in the New Testament sacrifice of the Redeemer consists precisely in His willingness to offer Himself. The blood of the animal offering atoned only symbolically, and had atoning power only as a temporary, figurative, typical substitution for a better offering, which is the mystic

background from which the divine permission of
animal sacrifice has gone forth. As the blood of the
animals which covered the floor of the court of the
priests indicated to Israel that it needed an atonement, so the veiled holy of holies, which was accessible
only to the high priest once a year, indicated that a
time must come when a sufficient atonement would be
furnished once for all, so that the presence of God
would no longer need to be concealed in such a
death-threatening manner, and so that the abode of
God would be accessible for all believers. But the
people of the legislation did not yet know that this
atonement was to be the voluntary sacrifice of a
man[1] whom God gives, and who gives himself in
death, to break the curse of sin through the moral
power of this act. In the age which now follows, the
Future One is not promised in the person of a sufferer
who offers himself, but in that of a prophet and king.

REMARK. — For the proper estimate of sacrifice,
the following considerations are decisive :—

1. Against the substitution theory of Baehr :[2] the
life of the sacrificial animal is not substituted by man
for his own life (נֶפֶשׁ), so that it is a symbol of it, but
it is a third somewhat which enters between God and
man for man.

2. Against the juristic theory of Kurtz: the

---

[1] Ex. xxxii. 30 : "And it came to pass on the morrow, that Moses
said unto the people, Ye have sinned a great sin : and now I will go
unto Jehovah ; peradventure I shall make an atonement for your sin."

[2] *Symbolik des Mosaischen Kultus*, in 2 vols., Heidelberg 1837–39.

slaughtering of the sacrificial animal is not a punitive
execution within the sacrificial ritual, that is, the
suffering of death as a punishment, but only the
means for securing the atoning blood, which is a type
of that poured out on Golgotha.   Hence the killing of
the sacrificial animal is never spoken of as a putting
to death (הֵמִית), but as a slaughtering (שָׁחַט or זָבַח).
In like manner the going up of the sacrifice in fire is
never called a burning (שָׂרַף), but a causing to ascend
in smoke (הִקְטִיר).

3. The sacrificial arrangement was a gracious one.
Atoning sacrifices were admissible for venial sins
(*peccata venialia*) alone, and only for mortal sins
(*peccata mortalia*) when grounds for mitigation made
them venial sins.   But on the day of atonement,[1]
year by year, the condition of the congregation as one
of grace is renewed.   The private and congregational
sacrifices during the year presuppose this annual
atonement of the congregation as such.

§ 28. *Moses and the Future Mediator.*

As the people were not able to bear the voice of
Jehovah in its awful nearness, and Moses was compelled to take the position of mediator between them
(Deut. v. 23–25 ; Ex. xx. 19), God also promised the
people for the future a prophet as mediator of the
divine revelation, like Moses, and demanded for him in

[1] See Delitzsch, *Der Versöhnungstag*, in Luthardt's *Zeitschrift für
Kirchliche Wissenschaft*, Leipzig 1880, pp. 173–183.

advance unconditional obedience (Deut. xviii. 15–19). Moses was not the only prophet of his age, but all prophecy beside him and after him moved in the realm created through his mediatorship. The one prophet in whom Moses' mediatorship finds its antitype as seen in the history of fulfilment, is the predicted Christ, who is here announced as a prophet. The prophets who arose between Moses and this one cannot be included in the expression, " a prophet like thee," for none of them was so great as Moses, according to the testimony of the Tora itself (Deut. xxxiv. 10 ; compare Num. xii. 6–8). None of them were mediators of such a divine revelation as the Sinaitic ; but that divine revelation, which will be like the Sinaitic, lies for all in the realm of the future.

REMARK.—The New Testament Scriptures see the promise of à prophet who is the antitype of Moses, fulfilled in Jesus (Acts iii. 22–24, vii. 37). Even among the Jewish people the knowledge dawned that the mighty and miraculous teacher from Nazareth " was the prophet that cometh into the world " (John vi. 14) ; but they did not know that the prophet of the Old Testament promise and the Messiah were one and the same person (John vii. 40 sq.; compare i. 19–21), although, beholding the person of Jesus, they surmised the identity of both.[1]

[1] Matt. xxi. 9–11, ver. 11 : "And the multitudes said, This is the prophet, Jesus, from Nazareth of Galilee."

§ 29. *The Beginning of Prophecy in the Time of Moses concerning the Future King.*

It is the result of different situations, that the image of the future mediator in the Sinaitic legislation takes on a prophetic image, and that in the mouth of Balaam it receives a special royal character,—in the mouth of that sorcerer whose magic Balak, the king of Moab, invokes against victorious Israel. The star and the sceptre, which Balaam sees going forth from Jacob-Israel (Num. xxiv. 17), signify, as emblems of the heavenly and earthly glory, the king in whom Jehovah's royal government over Israel [1] is humanly mediated. He is the king of the final period, through whom Israel conquers all the neighbouring nations; and though Israel for a time is threatened by Ashur, the world-empire of the East, and subjugated by Chittim,[2] the world-empire of the West (1 Macc. i. 1, viii. 5), it victoriously outlasts the nearest and most remote movements of the nations. Although occasioned by the circumstances of the age, this prophecy of Balaam, as the first properly Messianic prediction, forms an integral part in the systematic progress of revelation. That which is promised to Judah as the royal tribe is hereafter connected with the person of a king, through

[1] Num. xxiii. 21, last clause: "Jehovah their God is with them [*i.e.* Israel], and the shout of a king is among them." Num. xxiv. 7, last clause: "Their king shall be higher than Agag, and their kingdom shall be exalted."

[2] See Delitzsch, *Messianic Prophecies*, Edinburgh 1880, p. 41, Rem. 1.

whom Judah attains the dominion of the world, to which, according to Gen. xlix. 10, he was designated after the arrival in Shiloh.[1]

REMARK. — The king whom Balaam foresees is neither a succession of kings (that is, a *collectivum*),[2] nor is he David,[3] the victor over the Moabites and Ammonites. The one beheld is not this or that king who had already been (*vaticinium post eventum*), nor one like David in Balaam's nearer future, but the Future King who is exalted over all, through whom Judah attains the promised dominion over the world. For this cause Jeremiah (xlviii., xlix.) again takes up the prophetic threatenings against the neighbouring peoples as unfulfilled. Balaam's prophecy does not contain anything which is not fitting to his character and time. Schultz admits that it remains in tone and contents within the boundaries of Jacob's blessing.[4]

§ 30. *The Old Testament Object of Faith after the Testamentary Words of Moses.*

A great king and a great prophet are now hoped for; but their reciprocal relation is still concealed, and the personality of both is so far from being superhuman, that the desire for redemption is directed beyond both to Jehovah Himself. Hence in the great me-

[1] Compare Delitzsch, *ut supra*, p. 35 sq.

[2] See Hengstenberg, *Christologie des Alten Testaments*, 2d ed., Berlin 1854-57.

[3] Wellhausen, *Geschichte Israels*, Berlin 1878, p. 266.

[4] *Alttestamentliche Theologie*, Frankfort-on-the-Main 1878, p. 681.

morial song (Deut. xxxii.) neither the future prophet
nor the future king are thought of.   Jehovah is the
One who makes use of the heathen as instruments of
punishment against His people, and who, after He has
extinguished the rebellious mass, attests Himself to
the remnant as having compassion on them and as
avenging them, so that the history attains its goal in
the restoration of Israel, and in the uniting of all
nations in the praise of the God of Israel, who has
been revealed in judgment and mercy.   Even the
blessing of Moses (Deut. xxxiii.) deduces all salvation
from Jehovah, the eternal King, who is the refuge of
His people (compare Deut. xxxiii. 29 with Gen.
xlix. 18).   And the prayer of Moses (Ps. xc.) also takes
refuge in this God, since it recognises Him as the unchangeable One, as the Foundation of hope in danger
and death.   This faith, which hides itself in Jehovah,
seized at all times the redemption of Jesus Christ by
the root (compare Ps. cii. with Heb. i. 10–12).   As,
now, the younger generation stood on the threshold of
Canaan they hoped to see the great work of Jehovah's
salvation, which had been promised, but it became all
the while manifest that the essential, final redemption
had not yet appeared, and that the fulness of the
times must still be awaited.   Israel's entire history is
planned with the design that it should take refuge
from the God of the present in the God of the future,
who in the history of fulfilment becomes manifest as
the Father of Jesus Christ.

REMARK.—It would be impossible to conceive how

it is to be reconciled with the divine mercy, that God's love as revealed in the true salvation should be so long delayed, that the secret of the incarnation should be so long veiled, and that the image of the future Saviour should be formed in such a slow sporadic way, while at the same time retaining such a national externality, — all this, we say, would be inconceivable, if the faith which hides itself in Jehovah the God of Redemption had not been able at all times to seize the salvation of Jesus Christ by its root. It was therefore unavoidable for the Old Testament believers that the human mediation of salvation should recede as a mere accident behind the substance of Jehovah's work.

§ 31. *The Entrance on the Possession of the Land.*

When Israel entered into Canaan, it came the second time out of the waters. As at the creation the waters gave way that the firm land might appear, so now the waters of the Jordan gave way that Israel might secure a firm land. The conquest of Canaan occurred in connection with mighty miracles, as that part of the Book of Joshua which treats of the conquest (i.–xii.) relates. The conquest, indeed, as connected with the exodus from Egypt, forms the Old Testament redemption. But since the time of Joshua is the end of that work of God which commenced with the exodus, so too its miraculous glory is only a sunset. The miraculous presence of Jehovah in the cloudy

and fiery pillar has ceased. Bread has taken the
place of manna. The angel of Jehovah still appears,
but only seldom. The will of God is announced in
ordinary ways through the priesthood. In general, the
second half of the redemptive period, which ends with
the death of Joshua and Eleazar, is inferior to the first
half, ending with the death of Moses. It is true that
the part of the Book of Joshua which gives the
history of the distribution of the land, closes with the
thankful acknowledgment, Josh. xxi. 43–45: " And
Jehovah gave unto Israel all the land which He sware
to give unto their fathers . . . all came to pass."
But a larger portion of the land, especially the entire
sea-coast of Phœnicia and Philistia, was not yet
conquered, for only too soon Israel showed delay and
want of success in the continuation of the conquest,
which they had begun with energy, and placed themselves in the midst of all the dangers of apostasy,
which the destruction of the idolatrous population was
designed to prevent. This was the condition of affairs
when Joshua, shortly before his death, took an oath
from the people in Shechem that they would hold
fast to Jehovah.

REMARK.—We admit that there are miracles which
have arisen as legends, yet we do not deny the miracle
as a fundamental principle. But for this very reason
we need a criterium, so as to discriminate between
credible and incredible miracles. The display of such
extraordinary means as the interference of God in the
course of nature, only appears credible to us when

important ends of redemptive history are concerned ; and especially when they have to do, as in the time of Moses and Joshua, and in the time of Jesus and the apostles, with the foundation of a congregation of God for an entire world - age, hence with a creative beginning.

§ 32. *The Character of the Time of the Judges.*

Soon no more of the elders were left who had seen the miracles of the redemptive period. The people were like orphans. They answered with tears and sacrifices the divine message which admonished them to be faithful to God (Judg. ii. 1–5). This state of mind did not long continue. The heathen surroundings, with which Israel was hemmed in, decomposed its national consciousness, and relaxed the uniting bond of its religion. The tribe of Judah, during the time of the Judges, lost its pre-eminence. The history of the Judges is almost exclusively the history of the northern tribes. The separation between the north and the south became all the while more abrupt. One must not suppose that the dominion and activity of the Judges comprised the entire people. The unity of the people was broken, and their character was half Canaanitic. The time of the Judges resembles the age of chivalry. It was the time of Israelitish romance.

REMARK 1. — The Phœnician judges (*suffetes*), like the Roman consuls, stood two by two as independent magistrates at the head of the State. The Israelitish

judges, on the contrary, are called of God in an extraordinary manner to rescue Israel, and their activity
has rather an external than an internal direction.
They have in common with the prophets the extraordinary call, but are distinguished from them in this,
that their extraordinary mission was not of an ethico-
religious, but of a warlike nature.

REMARK 2.—Even Gideon, who had begun in the
spirit, ended in the flesh. Sampson presents a true
portrait of the Israel of that period. We see spirit
and flesh all the while contending in him, without the
spirit overcoming the flesh, and yet he is the Nazarite
of Jehovah, whose birth the angel announced with
words similar to those with which the angel Gabriel
announced the birth of Jesus Christ. The contrast
between both Testaments is here as great as possible.

§ 33. *The Footsteps of the Future One in the Time of the Judges.*

The course of the true seed of the woman went at
that time through the mire of great waters. The tribe
of Judah disappears so completely from the theatre of
history, that the song of Deborah does not mention it.
It is a law of redemptive history, that its ways, indicated by prophecy, suddenly appear as if they were
broken off, in order that they may come all the more
strikingly to view. The sacred historiography is conscious of this, for the Book of Judges begins with
divine oracle, implying the promise of victory (i. 2):
" Judah shall go up," and closes in xvii.-xxi. with

narratives which, revolving around Bethlehem-Judah, have as their frame the reflective remark, "In those days there was no king in Israel,"—by which it is indicated that the want of a legal kingdom is soon to be remedied, and that the beholding of the ways of God in the future is to be directed to Bethlehem-Judah. Hence the end of the Book of Judges is continued in the Book of Ruth. In this charming history of a family from Bethlehem-Judah, the coming Christ is far more prominent than in the warlike histories of the other tribes. As Ruth gleaned ears in the field of Boaz, God purposed through this daughter of a foreign land to give back the sceptre to the tribe of Judah, for the last word of the Book of Ruth is the name David.

REMARK 1.—Ancient writers regarded Judges and Ruth as one book. When Josephus (b. 37 A.D.), Melito of Sardis (d. about 170 A.D.), Origen (b. 185, d. 253 A.D.), Jerome (b. about 340, d. 420), reckon twenty-two books in the Old Testament, they consider Judges and Ruth as one. But the two narratives, Judg. xvii., xviii., xix.–xxi., and the history of the Book of Ruth, are most closely connected through their references to the tribe of Judah. From Bethlehem-Judah was the priest who arranged the tribal worship of the Danites. From Bethlehem-Judah was the wife of the Levite whose violation in Gibeah resulted in the annihilation of almost the entire tribe of Benjamin. From Bethlehem-Judah was Elimelech the husband of Naomi, who, with her daughter-in-law Ruth, the Moabitess, returned thither. The purpose of the Book of

Ruth is to relate the original history of the Bethlehem-itic family from which David came. There is no time which could have been more fitting for the composition of this book than the time of King Hezekiah. When Micah points to the roots of the parousia of the Messiah, which lie in the lowly community of Beth-lehem-Ephratah,[1] it seems as if the Book of Ruth was written to describe those ancient Bethlehemitic "goings forth."

REMARK 2.—The Book of Ruth relates a history from the time of the Judges, about one hundred years before David. The victorious song of Deborah belongs to a much earlier epoch of the time of the Judges, in which this is particularly significant, that it celebrates the miraculous revelation of God upon Mount Sinai (Judg. v. 4, 5): "Jehovah, when Thou wentest out from Seir, when Thou marchedst out from the fields of Edom, the earth trembled, also the heavens dropped, also the clouds dropped water. The mountains tottered before Jehovah, this Sinai before Jehovah, the God of Israel." These words of Deborah confirm Deut. xxxiii. 2 as Mosaic, and afford at the same time a parallel to the Book of Ruth, for the designation of God as Jehovah, God of Israel, is characteristic of the history of Joshua and of the Judges; compare Ruth ii. 12 with Judg. iv. 6, v. 3, 5, vi. 8, xi. 21–23, xxi. 3, 23.

[1] Micah v. 1 (E. V. ver. 2): "And thou Bethlehem-Ephratah, too small to be reckoned among the thousands of Judah, out of thee shall He go forth to me, who is to be ruler over Israel, and His goings out are from old, from the days of remote antiquity." Compare Delitzsch's *Messianic Prophecies*, Edinburgh 1880, pp. 44 sq.

§ 34. *The Messianic Hope in the Time of the Judges.*

How great the desire for a king was at that time
of dominant anarchy and barbarism, appears from the
prophecy of the man of God (1 Sam. ii. 27–36), which
announces the overthrow of the house of Eli, the high
priest in the line of Ithamar, and which promises a
priest after God's heart: " I will build him a reliable
house, and he shall walk before my anointed[1] for ever."
The same strong desire is seen in the song of Hannah
(1 Sam. ii. 1–10), who in the mirror of her elevation
from disgrace to honour beholds the triumph of the
oppressed congregation: " Jehovah, His adversaries
shall be broken in pieces; it thunders before Him in
heaven: Jehovah will judge the ends of the earth, and
will grant power to His king, and will exalt the horn
of His anointed."[2]   The prophecy of the man of God
was fulfilled in Zadok and Solomon, but was not
exhausted; and Hannah's song of praise began to be
fulfilled in David, but first drew near a final fulfilment
when, as it were, born again, it was re-echoed in
Mary's magnificat (Luke i. 46–55).

REMARK 1. — The prophecy, 1 Sam. ii. 27–36, is
considered by modern critics, since Ewald, Thenius, and
others, as a prediction after the event (*vaticinium post
eventum*), which has been interpolated in the old
history.   But we remark that it does not contain any-

---

[1] The Hebrew is לִפְנֵי־מְשִׁיחִי, which the Septuagint renders: ἐνώπιον
Χριστοῦ μου.

[2] Hebrew : קֶרֶן מְשִׁיחוֹ, Sept. κέρας Χριστοῦ αὐτοῦ.

thing which cannot be understood as a presage of the future at the end of the period of the Judges. The reliable priest is, according to the first fulfilment, as the Book of Kings itself remarks, that Zadok who took the place of Abiathar, because he entered into the conspiracy against Solomon in favour of Adonijah. Through Zadok the line of Eleazar again came into possession of the pontificate. Wellhausen, Smend, and W. Robertson Smith, indeed, think that Zadok was the founder of an absolutely new line, which did not belong to the house of Aaron, and that the genealogies of Chronicles, which refer his origin to Eleazar, are artificial inventions which are due to an unmistakable tendency.

REMARK 2.—The connection in which Hannah and David stand to each other is favourable to the genuineness of the song of Hannah. When Hannah had thus prayed, she consecrated the one to the Lord who was called to anoint the son of Jesse as king. Hannah, who was the songstress of Jehovah, became the mother of that Samuel who begat David, the founder of the poetry of the psalms, into the kingdom. The fact that the song of Hannah is very old is confirmed by this, that it had a fructifying influence upon all the later literature (compare 2 Sam. xxii. 32; Ps. lxxv. 6, 8).

§ 35. *Establishment of a New Age by Samuel.*

As Samuel established the first kings of Israel, and formulated the reciprocal rights and duties of the king and people (1 Sam. x. 25), so too he reorganized the prophetic office. Towards the end of the time of the Judges, prophecy became rare (1 Sam. iii. 1). But after the word of Jehovah came to Samuel in Shiloh, and then in Ramah, the people had in him the judge and at the same time the seer (1 Sam. ix. 9; compare 1 Chron. ix. 22, and elsewhere), and soon through him many others; for Samuel roused as with powerful electric strokes his contemporaries, who had come under the dominion of the flesh, and produced such a revival in Israel as they had never experienced before. The prophetic schools which he founded for the wakening and intensifying of the prophetic charism, became the nurseries of the literature of the regal period. Israelitish prophecy, according to Acts, dates from Samuel.[1]

REMARK.—As Saul came to Gibeah, a company of prophets moved down from the *bamah,* that is, a place of worship at Gibeah, before whom harp, tambourine, flute, and guitar were played (1 Sam. x. 5 sq. and verses 10–13). The messengers whom Saul sends to Ramah to take David meet a company of prophets at whose head is Samuel, and they fall into an ecstasy, as afterwards Saul himself (1 Sam. xix. 20–24). Here we

[1] Acts iii. 24: "Yea, and ll the prophets from Samuel, and them that followed after," etc.

meet with organized companies of prophets, who not only make excursions in order to secure a spiritual excitation, and meet together not only casually, but also have dwellings in common, which in Ramah, where the original society was, were called Newayoth or Nayoth. The music served to excite (2 Tim. i. 6) the prophetic charism. We have the same difficulty in obtaining a clear conception of this mode of prophecy, as of the gift of tongues in the primitive Church. It was so overpowering and exciting, that the auditor was irresistibly carried away by the power of the Spirit of God; so tempestuous, that the instruments did not drown it; and so violent, that Saul throws off his clothes, and remains lying on the ground as though caught away from this world. Since the power of the Divine Spirit expresses itself all the more powerfully in proportion as the natural life is lacking in spiritual character, the prophetic office of the time of the Judges is only a chaotic beginning. It has, like everything else in the time of the Judges, a Canaanite hue, a more mantic,[1] and so to speak Shamanian character.[2]   But Samuel was the man who in that barbarous age brought forth prophetism as the fruit of a great spiritual awakening. Those companies of prophets are an Old Testament Pentecostal phenomenon. As Abraham is the father of believers, and Moses is the

---

[1] Compare chap. iv. in Delitzsch's *Messianic Prophecies*, Edinburgh 1880, pp. 12–20.

[2] A picture of the wild self-excitement of the Shamans is given by Tholuck, who follows Castrin, in *Die Propheten und ihre Weissagungen*, Gotha 1860, § 1.

mediator of the law, so Samuel is the father of the kingdom and the prophetic office, and through the medium of the prophetic schools, father of the literature of the royal and prophetic period which now follows.

FOURTH PERIOD.

FROM THE FOUNDATION OF THE KINGDOM UNTIL ITS
DIVISION, THE PERIOD OF DAVID AND SOLOMON, OR
THE RISING AND SETTING OF THE ROYAL GLORY.

§ 36. *The Failure of the Benjaminitish Kingdom.*

A S from the commencement to the end of the
creation light was preceded by darkness, so in
the history of redemption the real beginnings of new
crises are mostly preceded by those which are abortive,
and which finally appear as the dark foil of the real.
Such an abortive beginning was Cain, the firstborn of
the seed of the woman, and Ishmael, the firstborn of
the seed of the patriarchs; such an one, too, was Saul,
the first king of Israel. For, while he was indeed the
chosen and anointed of Jehovah, yet he was the king,
after the pattern of the heathen, whom the people had
defiantly secured by the rejection of Jehovah's kingdom. He was not the man to blot out the stain of
the new beginning. But, also aside from Saul's un-
theocratic disposition, the new beginning was imperfect.
The office of judge (*shophet*), as represented by Samuel,
still continued, and the kingdom was almost exclusively
military. It was only a first step towards the right

form of the kingdom. On account of his autocratic behaviour in the war with Amalek, Samuel declared that Saul had forfeited the dominion. And from that time forth his nobler self was completely bound, he was attacked by a spirit of envy and melancholy, as if he were an usurper.

REMARK.—Saul's kingdom was not a pure gift of God, but he was nevertheless free, and according to 1 Sam. xiii. 13 the kingdom would have remained in his house if he had kept a theocratic disposition. But he did not keep it, and so divine government and human freedom interpenetrated to bring the history to the goal which God had decreed. Through Saul's disobedience, and his tragic end after the battle of Gilboa, the fleshly expectations of the people were punished, and room was made for the tribe of Judah, to which, from the beginning, the sceptre was promised.

§ 37. *David's Typical Way to the Throne.*

The luminous point whence, in the midst of this decadence, the true royal glory of Israel dawned, was Ramah. Here, in the school of the prophets at Nayoth, flourished under Samuel's fostering care poetry, music, and all the spiritual powers which were to become the satellites of the kingdom of promise. Thence Samuel was sent with the anointing horn to the house of Jesse in Bethlehem, that he might anoint the future king who was after God's heart. But David, although secretly anointed, was not a pretender. Saul was not abandoned by God until he entirely abandons himself. When David, through his victory over Goliath, had decided the war with the Philistines, Saul's love towards him was turned into envy and hatred. The night of persecution now begins, in which Saul's star gradually wanes before David's rising sun. As the future Christ of God is to be persecuted by the magistrates of His people unto death, but is thus advanced in His ascent to glory, so it was with David the present *christ* (anointed) of God. All his psalms from the time of persecution under Saul are typical, and even where the spirit of prophecy typically elevates the expressions of David concerning himself to prophecy (especially Ps. xxii.), the Messiah has no objectivity apart from David or above him. These psalms are Messianic on account of David's Messianic view of himself. He regarded himself as the Messiah of God,[1] although, through his experiences and words, he is only a means for representing the Future One before His coming.

REMARK.—After David's anointing there were two anointed ones of God; but all the hopes for redemption, cherished by believers, were directed towards the new kingdom which was in process of formation. David must have appeared to himself after his anointing in an entirely different light. He had now become the person to whom the longing expectation of the believers turned, and he must have appeared to himself of all the greater significance for the redemptive history, in proportion as he was joyfully conscious of

[1] Compare Delitzsch, *Messianic Prophecies*, Edinburgh 1880, p. 47.

the fullest devotion to the idea of his royal office.
The danger which threatens his life now threatens the
hope of Israel, and the light of Israel's future would
be extinguished together with his light.   On the
contrary, the expectation of his rescue is lost in
a most glorious perspective view of the future.   His
victory and triumph is that of all true Israel, and
his entrance into glory furnishes the material of
a proclamation which glorifies Jehovah among all
nations.   In all these Psalms of David the speaking
subject is not represented as a suffering righteous
man, but as the king of Israel who is passing [1]
through suffering (compare Ps. xxxi. 17, lxix. 18,
cix. 28, xxxv. 27, with lxi. 7).

§ 38. *The Elevation of David as Founder of the Kingdom of Promise.*

David was about eighteen years of age when he
was anointed by Samuel.   The time of persecution
under Saul lasted nearly a decade, for David was
thirty years old when he became king in Hebron over
Judah (2 Sam. v. 4).   Even his real kingdom has a
typically ascending scale.   Seven and a half years he
ruled only over Judah, and first after Ishbosheth's
murder, of which he was guiltless, he was anointed
king in Hebron over all Israel.   Throned in a newly
built palace, on Mount Zion, which he had taken from

[1] Compare Hengstenberg's *Commentar über die Psalmen*, Berlin
1849-1852.

the Jebusites, he was now planning, first of all, to
prepare a suitable place for the presence of Jehovah
in Israel.   He brought the ark from Kirjath-Jearim
to Zion into a tent-temple which had been erected
there, and then busied himself with a plan for building
Jehovah a fitting temple of cedar.   He then received
a decisive order from God through Nathan (2 Sam. vii.;
1 Chron. xvii.) declining his proposal, but requiting it
with the promise of an everlasting hereditary possession
of the throne under God's fatherly protection.   The
Messianic hope is henceforth linked with the house of
David, but the loss of glory, which he brings upon
himself through great sins, makes it evident to him
and the people that the Messianic hope is not to be
attached to his person.

REMARK.—It follows from 2 Sam. vii., 1 Chron. xvii.—

(1) That the king, who is to be the complete fulfilment of the hope of Israel, must be a son (descendant)
of David.

(2) That he will build the true temple of Jehovah,
a temple, as is clear at a later time, which is nobler
than the stone temple of Solomon, and that of the
post-exilic period, Zech. vi. 12.

(3) That the relation of the father to the son, in
which God places Himself to the king of the house of
David, will attain in the future ideal king its pro-
foundest depth and intimacy (Ps. ii. 7, 12).   The
seed of David, which is the object of the promise,
is not one ruler, but a chain of rulers.   Yet this seed
is to be understood like the collective " he " (הוא, Gen.

iii. 15, compare p. 25), which includes the Son of man *par excellence* as its centre and climax. Likewise the collective "he" (2 Sam. vii. 13, 14) includes in itself the Son of David in the highest sense, and the Founder of the true temple of God, which is the Church.

§ 39. *The Fate of the Messianic Hope.*

At the beginning of the very year in which David, by the victorious completion of the Syrio-Ammonitic war, attained the summit of external power, he plunged, through his adultery with Bathsheba, into the deepest misery. He is also, as betrayed by Ahithophel, still a type, but the persecution through Absalom belonged to the fourfold payment, which he had specified for himself (2 Sam. xii. 6); and the 110th Psalm, as well as his last words on his death-bed (2 Sam. xxiii. 1–7), show how, in consequence of his consciousness of his own guilt, the image of the Messiah was separated from his subjectivity, and came before him as a majestic form of the future. The prediction concerning the kingdom of the promise in Ps. lxxxix. 37 sq. is, that it shall continue as long as the sun and moon. But the sun of the house of David rises and sets, and the longing of the believers, so far as they expected a fulfilment in kings of the house of David, and especially in Solomon (1 Chron. xxii. 7–10, xxviii. 10, xxix. 1; 1 Kings v. 19, E. V. ver. 5, viii. 17–20), is disappointed again and again. The comfort of the

believers in this interchange of light and darkness is
Jehovah of Hosts, whose name is the characteristic of
the history of the kings, the God of the heavenly
hosts, whose fervent love will nevertheless work out
salvation, and will cause a sun to rise for the house of
Israel and the people of David which will never go
down again.

REMARK 1.—As David, betrayed by Ahithophel,
leaves Jerusalem accompanied by those of his com-
panions who had remained true to him; so Jesus,
betrayed by Judas, leaves Jerusalem accompanied
by those of His apostles who had remained faithful. David crosses the Kidron, and halts at one of
his favourite places on the mount of Olives, where
he was wont to pray [1] (2 Sam. xv. 32). As the sons
of Zeruiah begged for permission to take revenge on
Shimei, and David forbade him; so Jesus forbade the
sons of Salome, when they wished to take vengeance on
the Samaritans (Luke ix. 52–56); and as Ahithophel,
after the betrayal was accomplished, hanged himself;
so did Judas, when he saw that the fate of Jesus took
a different turn than he had anticipated. The Lord
Himself explains (John xiii. 18) that Ps. xli. 10 is fulfilled in the act of Judas Iscariot; and in John xvii. 12,
Acts i. 16, it is in general presupposed that the deed

---

[1] [2 Sam. xv. 30, 32: "And David went up by the ascent of *mount*
Olivet. . . . And it came to pass that when David was come to the
top of the *mount*, where he was wont to pray to God," etc. The
English version fails to express the idea of customary action which is
indicated by the imperfect יִשְׁתַּחֲוֶה.—C.]

and end of the traitor are predicted in the Old Testament Scriptures.

REMARK 2.—The 110th Psalm is characterized as prophetic through two oracular words of God, which elsewhere are unknown. There David calls the future Christ his Lord, and beholds in spirit the priestly and royal glory of the Conqueror of the world. The psalm rests on a typical foundation, but is prophetic, and hence directly Messianic. The last words of David (2 Sam. xxiii. 1–7) indicate that the expectation of the ideal Messiah will yet be realized within his house. He has the Future One before him as a righteous ruler among men, a ruler in the fear of God, whose dominion is like the rising of the sun, which fructifies the earth, on a cloudless morning.

REMARK 3.—The Messianic hope now progresses all the while further in such a form that, so far as it is attached to a king of the present or of the immediate future, it proves in every case to be deceptive. Through the contrast of the Davidic rulers with the ideal of the kingdom of promise, the Messianic hope is transferred more and more to the final period, and hence becomes eschatological. As sacrifice awakens a longing for the removal of the barriers which hinder an intercourse with God, so the kingdom awakens a longing after the truly anointed of God. For Messianic prophecy always gains in intensity, when the present incumbent of the kingdom is a caricature of its ideal.

REMARK 4.—God is called Jehovah of Hosts, not

as commander of the armies of His people,[1] but as
commander of the heavenly armies;[2] for of twenty-
nine places which speak of the hosts of Israel, twenty
belong to the Pentateuch, and yet this name of God
is unknown in the Pentateuch, including the Books of
Joshua and Judges. It first appears in 1 Sam. i. 3,
hence on the threshold of the history of the kingdom.
Thus interpreted, it signifies the God of omnipotent
power in heaven, who victoriously accomplishes His
work of salvation. The *gloria* of the heavenly hosts
at the birth of Christ shows what meaning the name
has, and to what goal it points.

§ 40. *Retrospective View of David's Personality.*

The fundamental trait in David's character is a
deep and tender susceptibility, which, although even
for a time it may yield to lust or the pressure of the
world, yet always quickly rises up again in repentance and faith, and the fundamental trait of his time
is a rapid succession of tribulations and consolations, of
exaltations and humiliations. David's poetry of the
psalms has arisen from a disposition at one time elegiac,
at another hymnic, which has been occasioned by these
abrupt transitions. In his psalms, which are the fruits
of his external and internal struggles, he is the immortal witness to the old as well as to the Christian world

[1] See Schrader in the *Jahrbücher für protestantische Theologie*,
Leipzig 1875.
[2] Compare Delitzsch, *Lutherische Zeitschrift*, Leipzig 1874, pp.
217-222.

(Isa. lv. 4). The poetical gifts of Asaph and the sons of Korah, although they are so peculiar, have been kindled by David. His psalms unite in themselves the prophetic stamp of the Asaphic and the priestly character of the Korahitic. In general, the offices of king, prophet, and priest are united in no Old Testament person to any such extent as in David. And yet the typical significance of the beginning of the kingdom of promise is not exhausted in him; David's typical character is supplemented by that of Solomon.

REMARK 1.—The psalms are the fruit of the working of the Divine Spirit, under which David was placed after his anointing; but there are, besides, two other productions which indicate his noble and sanctified humanity,—

(1) The elegy over Saul and Jonathan (2 Sam. i. 19–27). As in view of the remains of a friend all the pain which he caused us while living is forgotten in the remembrance of his excellences, and the kindness which he showed us, so David no longer has a memory for the period of persecution now past. He is a man, and not the judge of the dead. Therefore Saul stands before him only in his virtues, and he celebrates not only Jonathan, but also Saul, as loved ones who can never be forgotten. We see in this case that anger belongs only to the accidental utterances of noble souls, whose constant motive is love. David's noble and sanctified humanity is also manifested—

(2) In his lament for Abner (2 Sam. iii. 33 sq.). It must have seemed to David, from a prudential point

of view, that Abner's death was a piece of good fortune. But the strength of his moral indignation does not suffer itself to be assuaged by worldly considerations. He openly and decidedly frees himself from all complicity with the villanous deed. He curses Joab, who assassinated Abner, follows Abner's bier, and lingers weeping and fasting at his grave until sunset.

REMARK 2.——It also appears elsewhere in the history of salvation that two persons or things form together a pair (syzygy), since they represent the two correlated sides of the future; as, for example, Elijah and Elisha are types of the suffering and the glory of the future Prophet; Joshua and Zerubbabel are types of the future priestly King; the goat designed for sacrifice on the altar (Lev. xvi. 15 sqq.), and the azazel goat (Lev. xvi. 26) of the day of atonement, are types of the future imputative and actual putting away of sin; such a pair of types are also David and Solomon.

§ 41. *The Character of Solomon and of his Age.*

David is the type of the course of Christ through humiliation to glory, and Solomon (1 Kings i.–xi.; 2 Chron. i.–ix.) is the type of this glory itself. He is the man of rest,[1] as his name indicates. His time was the most fortunate for Israel. Never did Israel take a more respected position among the nations, never did

_____
[1] 1 Chron. xxii. 9: "Behold, a son shall be born to thee, who shall be a man of rest; and I will give him rest from all his enemies round about: for his name shall be Solomon, and I will give peace and rest unto Israel in his days."

it stand to them in such a peaceful intercourse of material and intellectual interchange. Israel saw itself placed at that time in such a fulness of relations to the world, in riches and elements of culture, as it had never experienced before; and Solomon, with a high consciousness of his nationality, knew how to master these relations to the world without surrendering anything of Israel's honour. His æsthetic taste knew how to transform these riches into a beautiful adornment for his court, Jerusalem, and his empire. His wisdom (1 Kings iii. 7) knew how to unite these elements of culture into a whole which was permeated by the religion of Jehovah. Israel under Solomon was carried beyond itself to become a type of the Church, which is freed from its Old Testament barriers, and spiritually rules the world.

REMARK.—Phoenicia and Egypt, the abodes and the laboratories of inherited wisdom and art, were at that time kingdoms connected with Israel on close terms of friendship. Hiram was Solomon's friend, and a daughter of Pharaoh was his wife. The ships of Israel at that time went from the Red Sea to Tarshish, that is, Tartessus in Hispania baetica, and to Ophir, which is (according to Lassen's probable conjecture) on the shore of Abhira, between the delta of the Indus and the gulf of Cambay, and brought from thence the products and learning of strange lands, which had been previously closed to Israel.

§ 42. *Characteristics of the Chokma.*

The tendency of the age of Solomon in relation to the tendency of that of David, may be compared to the tendency of Alexandrian Judaism in relation to that of the Palestinian.   It is directed to the human, the ideal, and the universal elements in Israel's religion and history, and connects the essence of the Israelitish religion with the elements of truth in heathenism. As knowledge (*gnosis*) goes forth from faith (*pistis*), so the age of Solomon is the new age of wisdom (*chokma*), which has gone forth from the age of David.   While prophecy serves the process of redemptive history, chokma hastens on before it, and anticipates the universal ideas, through which the adaptation of the religion of Jehovah to become the religion of the world is recognised.   The Book of Proverbs, the Book of Job, and Solomon's Song are products of this intellectual, and, to a certain degree, philosophical tendency.   In the Book of Proverbs the name of Israel nowhere occurs, but that of man (*adam*) is found all the more frequently. The hero of the Book of Job is a personal and actual proof of the grace which is also active outside of Israel, and the entire book is a protest against the legal pride of orthodox Phariseeism, which, having run fast into the dogma of retribution, is not able to keep sin and suffering apart.   And Solomon's Song is a circle of dramatic pictures which place before our eyes the love of man and woman in its monogamous and divinely sanctified ideality.   All these three books

treat of the relation of man, as such, to God and man.
From this we perceive how little there is that is
specifically Israelitic in the Solomonic literature.

REMARK 1.—We see the preparation for this largeness of heart, and for the removal of the husk of
nationality from humanity in the Psalms; for (1) in
them the desire is expressed in many ways that the
heathen may be drawn into the fellowship of salvation;
and (2) in them the ceremonial of the Tora is already
broken in pieces, so that the spirit does not recognise
it at all except as symbolic. Samuel gave expression
to a thought which in this respect can be considered
as one of the productive germs of the poetry of the
Psalms, 1 Sam. xv. 22, 23 : "Hath Jehovah as great
delight in burnt-offerings and sacrifices as in obeying
the voice of Jehovah? Behold, to obey is better than
sacrifice, to hearken than the fat of rams; for disobedience is the sin of witchcraft, and stubbornness is
teraphim-wickedness." [1]

REMARK 2.—There are scarcely two books which furnish a greater contrast in their contents than Solomon's
Song and the Book of Job; the former bounds like a
gazelle in the spring-time and sunshine, the latter wades
through the mire of deep suffering and enigma; and
between them the Book of Proverbs moves with a
cheerful earnestness through the "vanity fair" of life.
But all three books are of one character. They are
not specifically Israelitic, but place themselves upon

---

[1] This translation rests upon an amended reading proposed by some
critics which omits the connective before תְּרָפִים in ver. 23.—C.

the basis of pure humanity.   The allegorical interpretation of Canticles makes Solomon a prophet or a mystic, but he was neither the one nor the other.

REMARK 3.—The epos and the drama are peculiar to the Indo-Germanic race. The peoples of Islam first received epics and dramas through the Persians, who were converted to Islam; but in the time of Solomon the Israelitish literature was removed only a step from the development of the drama. The Song of Solomon and the Book of Job are dramas: the one, even as the ancients called it, is a comedy, the other a tragedy. But the one stills lies in the swaddling-clothes of lyric poetry, and the other in the swaddling-clothes of historiography. The Book of Job also resembles the classic tragedy in other respects. Job is a tragic hero. He maintains an unshaken consciousness of his innocence before the decree which crushes him like fate. But the result of the drama is not here, as in the ancient tragedies, that the fate destroys him, but that Job's idea of the fate (*decretum absolutum*) itself, that is, his false conception of God, is annihilated as a phantom of temptation.

§ 43. *The Building of the Temple.*

The crowning point of Solomon's glory was the day when the temple was dedicated.   Even in his dedicatory prayer, joy, freedom, and largeness of heart prevail in his view of divine and human things, which is peculiar to that time of peace (1 Kings viii. 22–53,

especially vers. 37–40). Jehovah made Himself known
in wonderful manifestations of His presence to this
temple, which was founded with the intent that it
should become a house of prayer for all nations
(1 Kings viii. 10–12; 2 Chron. vii. 1–3). The
wandering tent had now become a fixed palace. But
Jehovah did not consent to this palatial building
without reluctance; and although Solomon sees in it
the fulfilment of the promise (1 Kings viii. 12–21),
yet this magnificent building of hewn stone and
cedars, in which Phœnician art had participated to as
great a degree as Israelitish incitement and work,
could not possibly be the house that the promise
finally had in view; hence the history of Israel
immediately takes a turn, which aims at destroying
this glory, since it is still only cosmical, and is incongruous with the gracious thoughts of God.

REMARK. — In the prayer which Solomon utters
before the altar, with hands raised toward heaven, he
prays, among other things, if any kind of plague
burdens the land, that then Jehovah, as knowing the
hearts, may answer every suppliant as it seems good
to Him, even those who are not Israelites, who come
thither to pray, "that all peoples of the earth may
know Thy name, may fear Thee like Thy people
Israel" (vers. 37–40). Jehovah acknowledged even
this temple. The cloud of His glory filled it, so
that Solomon said, setting forth and praising the
majestic mystery, "Jehovah hath determined to
dwell in thick darkness" (1 Kings viii. 12). But all

indications of God's gracious presence were only an accommodated condescension in accordance with the educational plan of the divine love. When the stone letter of the law shall once become spiritualized, then, too, this stone temple is to give way to a spiritual temple of living stones (1 Pet. ii. 4 sq.), and therefore the history of Israel immediately takes a turn in the direction of this goal.

§ 44. *The Division of the Kingdom.*

It is a law of every earthly thing, that when it has once attained the height of its completion, it disappears like a fleeting shadow of the Eternal. The Solomonic glory at its culmination carried in itself the germs of decay. The consequences which the Mosaic law was designed to preclude by shutting off Israel from the nations, and prohibiting the king from the luxury of Oriental rulers (Deut. xvii. 14 sqq.; compare 1 Sam. x. 25), were not prevented. Moreover, the old envy of the tribes of Joseph still smouldered beneath the ashes. Even under David it had found vent for itself in the hostile and repeated demonstrations of the tribe of Benjamin. But Solomon not only did nothing to hinder the danger of a division of the kingdom, he even brought it on, since he cultivated a feeling which was favourable to desires for a false freedom, and at the same time he increased to the utmost the dissatisfaction with the burden of work and taxation occasioned through boundless luxury in the maintenance of his court. An inward voice did not leave him in uncertainty concerning what was impending (1 Kings xi. 9–13). Even while he yet lived there went forth from that very Shiloh, whence the blessing of Jacob had dated the world-empire of Judah, the prophet Ahijah, who tore the government of Judah in pieces, and took from him ten tribes of his own people.

REMARK.—The law of the king (Deut. xvii. 14 sq.) is now held to have been occasioned by the luxury of the Davidic court after Solomon, and that its form was determined by these circumstances. But after all, this can only be said of the prohibition, which forbids the king to multiply wives, horses, and treasures. Yet a motive is given for the warning against multiplying horses—that he may not lead the people back again to Egypt—which can scarcely be understood otherwise than as from the Mosaic age;[1] and we may therefore believe that this law of the king is essentially Mosaic, and that perhaps even Samuel's law of the kingdom[2] was based on Mosaic foundations.

[1] Compare Delitzsch, *Der Gesetzkodex des Deuteronomium*, in Luthardt's *Zeitschrift*, Leipzig 1880, p. 564 sq.

[2] 1 Sam. ix. 25 : "Then Samuel told the people the law of the kingdom, and wrote it in a book, and laid it up before Jehovah," etc.

FIFTH PERIOD.

FROM REHOBOAM AND JEROBOAM I. UNTIL THE END OF
THE DIVIDED KINGDOM. THE PERIOD OF ISRAEL'S
CONFLICTS WITH THE WORLD - EMPIRES, AND OF
PROPHECY, WHICH HOVERS OVER BOTH STATES UNTIL
THEIR FINAL CATASTROPHE.

§ 45. *The Four Epochs and their Two Characteristic Powers.*

THIS period, which lasts nearly four hundred years, is divided into the following four epochs:—

First Epoch: From the contemporaneous reigns of Rehoboam and Jeroboam I. to the contemporaneous reigns of Asa and Ahab, that is, the four last years of Asa's reign and the three first of Ahab's (975–915 B.C.).

Second Epoch: From the contemporaneous reigns of Jehoshaphat and Ahab to those of Amaziah and Jeroboam II., that is, the last fifteen years of Amaziah's reign and the first fifteen of Jeroboam's (914-811 B.C.).

Third Epoch: From the contemporaneous reigns of Uzziah and Jeroboam II. to the fall of the kingdom of Israel, that is, until the sixth year of Hezekiah's reign (810–722 B.C.).

Fourth Epoch: From the seventh year of Hezekiah's

reign until the fall of the kingdom of Judah (721–586 B.C.).

World-empire and prophetism are from this time forth the main factors in redemptive history. While God makes the world-empires the means of punishing and disciplining His people, prophecy raises itself at the same time announcing God's wrath, and in the midst of wrath comforting His people with His love. Henceforth these two factors give Israel's history its peculiarity and movement. The prophets represent the true spiritual character of the law. They represent that pragmatism of the history of Israel which is for ever established in Deut. xxxii., and xxviii.-xxx., Lev. xxvi. And in proportion as Israel's history becomes interwoven with the world's history, the prophet's horizon and mission are expanded.

REMARK 1.—World-empire is a political, and at the same time an ethical idea. As a political idea, it indicates a kingdom whose circuit is almost co-extensive with the entire ancient civilised world. The name is the translation of *civitas mundi, monarchia mundi,* for which Sleidan (b. 1506, d. 1556) uses *imperium summum,*[1] and is certainly hyperbolic. The distinguishing characteristic of the world-empire is the lust for conquest, which seeks to subdue the entire world; and a means of subjugation which is peculiar to it is the expatriation of rebellious peoples from their native lands. As an ethical conception, world-empire

---

[1] His work, *De quatuor summis Imperiis,* first appeared in Strassburg, 1556.

is the world-power in which the worldly dominion and
civilisation which are antagonistic to the kingdom of
God culminate.   We have already seen that the city
of Cain was the beginning of this world-empire (*civitas
mundi*) ; Rome is the last link in this chain.[1]

REMARK 2. — The Judæan succession of kings
reckons ninety-five years from the division of the
kingdom until Jehu and Athaliah contemporaneously
assumed royal power, and the Israelitic ninety-eight
years.   From that point until the fall of Samaria, in
the sixth year of Hezekiah, the succession of the kings
of Judah embraces one hundred and sixty-five years ;
that of Israel, one hundred and forty-four.   These
differences admit of a reconciliation through the
assumption of co-regencies (2 Kings xv. 5) and of
interregnums.   But the synchronism of the Judæan
and of the Babylonio-Assyrian history lays before us
hard riddles.   The latter chronology is found in the
canon of Ptolemæus, in the eponymous lists of Assyria,
and in the annals of Sargon and Sennacherib.   Here
the relation between the two modes of chronology is
still the subject of investigation, but the following
dates can be considered as fixed almost beyond con-
troversy :—722 or 721 B.C., the fall of Samaria ; 625,
accession of Nabopolassar to the throne; 604, accession

---

[1] Compare Delitzsch's *Messianic Prophecies*, Edinburgh 1880, pp.
62-65, where it is affirmed that "the world-empire, beginning with
Assyria, becomes the inheritance at one time of this, at another
time of that dominant people, finally of the Romans," and it is implied
that the Roman world-empire still exists in fact as the world-power,
although no longer under this old name.—C.

of Nebuchadnezzar; 587 or 586, fall of Jerusalem; 537, release of the exiles by Cyrus.

§ 46. *The Relation of the Prophets to the Political and Religious Division.*

The division of the kingdom was foretold by Ahijah as a divine punishment. It took place, therefore, by divine right (*jure divino*); hence Shemaiah, as Rehoboam arms himself against Jeroboam, comes between them, and the reunion of the tribes is not demanded by any prophet of either kingdom as a duty, but is only considered a future work of God. Yet the case with the religious division which immediately followed the political, is entirely different; for out of dynastic considerations Jeroboam sought to perpetuate the independence of his dominion by destroying the religious unity of both kingdoms, and by introducing a new mode of worship, which, without cutting loose from Jehovah, met the heathen lusts and Egyptian propensities of the masses through the choice of a symbol derived from the Egyptian steer-god, and flattered the Ephraimitic national pride by the choice of ancient places celebrated through the great national reminiscences connected with them (1 Kings xii. 26 sqq.; Amos iv. 4, v. 5, viii. 14; Hos. iv. 15). This syncretistic state religion (Amos vii. 10, 13), with its self-created priesthood, and its servile, fawning prophets, is considered by the prophets of Jehovah in both kingdoms as an accursed apostasy; and so every fraternization of the kings of Judah with the kings of Israel excites the displeasure of the prophets, even when it is favourable to the interests of the kingdom of Judah.   Hence in the kingdom of Israel one royal family after another is smitten by the punitive prediction of the prophets, and is removed.   In the kingdom of Judah such a change of dynasties was impossible; for the Davidic dynasty rested on an unqualified promise, and the regulations rendered sacred by law and promise were there recognised as legally valid, so that the bad reality was deservedly self-condemned; this self-condemnation is mediated by the prophets.   They are the conscience of the state, but how mightily this conscience had to beat in Judah begins to appear even in the portraiture of the morals of Rehoboam and his age in colours which are black as night (1 Kings xiv. 21–24).

§ 47. *The Preformative Character of the First Epoch.*

First in view of the destruction of the people's unity, the prophetic office, which had been dumb for forty years, reappeared.   The Solomonic period moves on the level heights of prosperity and possession, but after the partition of the kingdom, Israel's way goes, although for a few centuries upwards and downwards, nevertheless steadily down into the depths of the Assyrian and Babylonian banishment, and in this way prophecy is given to accompany the people as a preacher of God's counsel, which, in spite of error and judgment, will nevertheless be actualized.   The physiognomy of the people's history remains essentially similar until the twofold catastrophe.   Nothing occurs in the following epochs which had not been prepared and delineated even in the first.   The prophets of both kingdoms in the first epochs are, in their doing and suffering, forerunners and prototypes of the latter, *e.g.* Hanani, 2 Chron. xvi. 7–10, compare Isa. vii.; and the man of God, 1 Kings xiii., compare Amos vii. 10 sqq.   The prophetic preaching had not yet at that time the subsequent oratorical perfection, but even then the prophecy of the first period was busied with the recording of the history of the time, and this prophetic historiography is really the source from which the literature of the properly prophetic books has been gradually developed.

REMARK.—The same Pharaoh Sheshonk I. (שִׁישַׁק), the founder of the twenty-second dynasty, who was Jeroboam's patron, made war against Judah, and plundered the temple and palace.   This event, which is a prelude to the Chaldæan catastrophe, is bewailed by Ethan the Ezrahite (1 Kings v. 11, compare 1 Chron. ii. 6) in Ps. lxxxix.   Even yet the image of Rehoboam is to be seen on the walls of the old royal palace of Egyptian Thebes (now Karnak).   The Jewish lineaments are not to be mistaken.   He is here presented to posterity as conquered by Egypt.

§ 48. *The Israelitish Prophets of the Second Epoch.*

In the second epoch (914–811 B.C.) falls the activity of Elijah, under the kings Ahab and Ahaziah, and of

Elisha, under Joram, and under Jehu and Joash, with whom, after the dynasty of Omri, the mightiest and most enduring dynasty of the northern kingdom begins. Along with the prophets of the Jeroboamic worship, and with those of the worship of Baal and Astarte, which the Phœnician Jezebel had introduced, there were at that time also in the northern kingdom prophets of Jehovah like Micaiah the son of Imlah (1 Kings xxii.). These prophets of Jehovah are all surpassed by Elijah the Tishbite, and by Elisha of Abel-meholah, through whom the power and glory of Jehovah was manifested in great miracles in opposition to the dominant half-heathenism founded by Jeroboam, and the entire heathenism introduced by Jezebel. The life of Elijah represents the struggle of prophetism, and that of Elisha its triumph. Elijah wrestles unto blood with the idolatrous house of Omri, and its prophets and priests. Elisha only executes the curse which Elijah had laid upon the house of Omri, and then stands by the house of Jehu in high honour. Elijah is like the embodiment of the divine anger, and Elisha is like the embodiment of the divine blessing; and since to be persecuted by the world unto blood is esteemed by God more highly than to be honoured by the world, Elijah, who consumed himself in fiery zeal (compare Sirach xlviii. 1), is caught up in fire to heaven, but Elisha goes the way of all flesh, although not without having the power of life still manifested on his bones.

REMARK.—The following four dynasties held the royal power in Israel during the second epoch :—

(1) The dynasty of Jeroboam: he reigned twenty-two years, and his son Nadab two years. Nadab was murdered by Baasha.

(2) The dynasty of Baasha: he reigned twenty-four years, and his son Elah two years. Elah was assassinated by Zimri, who maintained his power only seven days, and was put out of the way by Omri, who was elected by the people as king.

(3) The dynasty of Omri: he reigned for twelve years, during a part of which time Tibni was a rival king. Omri's son Ahab reigned twenty-two years, and was succeeded by his son Ahaziah for two years, and then by his second son Joram for twelve years, who was slain by Jehu.

(4) The dynasty of Jehu: he reigned twenty-eight years, his son Jehoahaz seventeen years, Jehoahaz's son Jehoash sixteen years, succeeded by his son Jeroboam II., who reigned forty-one years, followed by his son Zacariah, who was slain by Shallum, son of Jabesh, after a reign of six months. Shallum maintained the royal power only a month. The Joash mentioned above, the grandson of Jehu, is the one who wept over Elisha at his last illness.

§ 49. *The Judæan Prophets of the Second Epoch.*

The contemporaneous prophetical office of the kingdom of Judah did not accomplish any violent and mighty acts. Its activity consists in a fearless testimony against the fraternization of the two royal houses, and against idolatry.

Such testimonies were given against the alliance of the royal houses by Jehu, the son of Hanani, the seer, under Jehoshaphat king of Judah, and Ahab king of Israel (2 Chron. xix. 1–3), and by an anonymous prophet under Amaziah (2 Chron. xxv. 7–10); and against idolatry by Zechariah, the son of Jehoiada, under Joash (2 Chron. xxiv. 17–22), and by an anonymous prophet in the time of Amaziah (2 Chron. xxv. 15 sq.). The prophets were also bearers of the promise of victory for the encouragement of the people, when they were in need of comfort and deserved it. Such was Jahaziel, the son of Zechariah, under Jehoshaphat (2 Chron. xx. 14–17). The completest unity of spirit existed between the prophets of both kingdoms (compare 2 Chron. xxii. 7).[1] The letter of Elijah to Jehoram of Judah (2 Chron. xxi. 12–15) shows that a keen interest of the prophets of Israel in the destiny of the sister kingdom was presupposed; and what recognition the Israelitish prophets found in Judah appears from the religious significance which Elijah won in the consciousness of the Jewish people, for until the present day it is customary at the ceremony of circumcision to place a seat for him as an invisible guest. In Elijah the prophetic schools had gained a second Samuel as

[1] The Book of Kings is a work of prophetical historiography, and the Judæan author considers the judgment which Jehu executed against the house of Omri, and which also befell Ahaziah the king of Judah, as a divine decree. Compare, on the other hand, how Hosea (i. 4) regards the bloody deed of Jehu after he had shown that he was an unworthy instrument of God.

their head.   They now reappear in the foreground of
history.   Even that Jehu, son of Hanani, who prophesied to the house of Baasha its downfall (1 Kings
xvi. 1–4), was, according to 2 Chron. xx. 34, author
of a history of King Jehoshaphat.

REMARK.—Jehoshaphat, who reigned twenty-five years,
was followed by his son Joram, who ruled eight years,
and was perhaps a co-regent with his father (2 Kings
viii. 16).   Joram radically disappointed the wishes
and expectations uttered in Ps. xlv., which seem to
have been expressed on the day of his marriage.[1]   His
wife was Athaliah, the daughter of Jezebel.   He was
succeeded by his son Ahaziah, who reigned one year,
and who, together with the remaining members of the
house of Jehu, was slain by Omri (2 Kings viii. 29,
ix. 27).   Then followed the dreadful rule of Athaliah
for six years.   All the members of the Davidic house
were massacred, with the exception of Joash, who
alone was rescued, and was secretly reared in the
temple by Jehoiada the high priest; and when he was
seven years of age he was presented to the people as
the legitimate king, and Athaliah was slain.   This
Joash reigned fourteen years, and as a pious king so
long as Jehoiada stood at his side as a mentor; after
that he degenerated, until he became a murderer of
the prophets.   In the first half of Joash's reign the

[1] See Delitzsch's *Commentary on Psalms*, Edinburgh 1871, *in
loco*, where he maintains that this psalm is an epithalamium composed in honour of the marriage between Joram and Athaliah, and
expresses the Messianic hopes which were connected with the accession
of the son of Jehoshaphat.—C.

prophet Joel appeared; Joel is somewhat younger than Obadiah.

§ 50. *Obadiah and Joel.*

Under Joram, Jerusalem was given a second time into the hands of the heathen (2 Chron. xxi. 16 sq.; compare 1 Kings xiv. 25 sq.). The apostasy of Edom, and the plundering of Jerusalem at that time, which was a prelude to the Chaldæan catastrophe, in so far as a part of the Judæan people then became exiles, was the occasion of the literature of prophecy which began with Obadiah. Its first monument is a fugitive leaf against Edom, which, however, contains all the themes of prophecy in the time of the world-empires : Jehovah's judgment against the heathen; Israel's deliverance and the redemption of the world under the dominion of the victorious God of Israel.

Somewhat later, in one of the first thirty years of King Joash (about 860 B.C.), Joel appeared, who refers to Obadiah.[1] He outdoes the two promises which concern the immediate future respecting the destruction of the locusts and the outpouring of the rain, by the eschatological promises of the outpouring of the Spirit upon all flesh, and the judgment upon the hostile nations in the valley of Jehoshaphat. The prophet

[1] The passage which Professor Delitzsch thinks is directly referred to by Joel is verse 17 of Obadiah : "But upon Mount Zion shall be deliverance," etc. ; comp. Joel iii. 5 : "For upon Mount Zion and in Jerusalem shall be deliverance, as Jehovah hath said [*i.e.* by Obadiah], and in the remnant whom the Lord shall call."—C.

himself is the teacher of righteousness (ii. 23).[1]
Obadiah prophesies, in ver. 21, the coming of saviours;
but in Joel the final acts of salvation appear
as Jehovah's own work, without thought of human
intervention.[2]

REMARK.—In Obadiah, whose age is that of Lycurgus
(ninth century B.C.) and of Joel, Greece already enters
into the history of Israel, for Sepharad (סְפָרַד, ver. 20),
where exiles from Jerusalem are placed, is probably
Sparta, as city or country, perhaps as the home of the
Dorians in Asia Minor. Joel says, in respect to the
same event (iii. 6), that the inhabitants of Judah and
Jerusalem were sold as slaves to the Grecians (בְּנֵי
הַיְּוָנִים). In the Persian cuneiform inscriptions of
Behistun and Nakshi Rustem, Çparda and Juna stand
together. The bringing down of Joel into the past
exilic age[3] by Duhm,[4] Merx,[5] Stade,[6] and others, is
one of the most rotten fruits of the modern criticism.

---

[1] We translate: "For He has given you the instructor unto righteousness, and has caused to come down for you the rain, and the latter
rain in the first month," that is, from this time forth. The English
version is here objectionable, because it gives the rendering, "and He
will cause," contrary to the traditional text, and is moreover tauto-
logical.

[2] For the relation of Obadiah's prophecy to the Messianic idea, see
Delitzsch's *Messianic Prophecies*, Edinburgh 1880, p. 57.—C.

[3] Comp. Delitzsch's *Messianic Prophecies*, Rem. 3, p. 110.—C.

[4] Duhm, *Die Theologie der Propheten*, Bonn 1875.

[5] Merx, *Die Prophetie Joel und ihrer Ausleger*, Halle 1879.

[6] Stade, *De populo Javan*, academical Programme with Latin title,
but written in German, Giessen 1880. Compare the articles by
Delitzsch in the *Lutherische Zeitschrift*, Leipzig 1851; *Wann weis-
sagte Obadia?* p. 91; and *Zwei sichere Ergebnisse im Betreff der Weis-
sagungsschrift Joels*, p. 306.

§ 51. *The Doctrine and the Type of Jonah's History.*

Obadiah and Joel are contemporaries of Elisha, nevertheless without having any relation to him; but Jonah, son of Amittai, may have proceeded from the school of Elisha, who, according to 2 Kings xiv. 25, had prophesied the restoration of the kingdom of Israel to its promised extent (Deut. iii. 17, iv. 49), a prophecy which was fulfilled by Jeroboam II.[1]   We see from this how very much the prophetism of the northern kingdom was at that time turned from the Messianic hope which had been connected, through the prediction in 2 Sam. vii., with the house of David.   Nevertheless it becomes evident that all which was prophesied of the participation of other nations with Israel in the redemption, sprung from the depth of the divine decree, and not from the nature of the people.   This clearly appears from the Book of Jonah.   The commission to preach to the Ninevites, and to bring the heathen city to repentance through the preaching of judgment, and the thought of their finding pardon, are insupportable to the prophet.   It requires divine interference to bring him to the accomplishment of the commission, and to make him ashamed of his narrow-minded sulkiness.   But the conduct of the prophet is only the dark foil of this wonderful

---

[1] Some German commentators see in Isa. xv. xvi. this old prophecy of Jonah, which, according to Isa. xvi. 13, as they think, has been reproduced by Isaiah.   But it is sufficient for the refutation of this hypothesis that Moab (Isa. xvi. 1) is summoned to send tribute to Jerusalem.   Nowhere does a trace appear that the conquering people, which overcomes Moab, is the Israel of the northern kingdom.

book, which strengthens the universality of the redemption in the face of Jewish exclusiveness, not only with prophetic words, but through the facts of the prophet's history. We know, from Matt. xii. 39–41, and Luke xi. 30, what a far-reaching type Jonah's passage through a three days' sojourn in the belly of the fish is.[1]

REMARK.—The motive which drives Jonah to take a course diametrically opposed to God's commission is just that particularism which was active among the Jews of Pisidian Antioch (Acts xiii. 44 sq., compare 1 Thess. ii. 16), and from which even Peter, when he was to enter a heathen house with the preaching of redemption, had to be freed by a heavenly vision (Acts xi.). The Book of Jonah is an anticipation of this divine decision about seven centuries before, for the sending of Jonah to Nineveh probably falls in the time of the decline of the Assyrian empire under one of the kings, before his re-elevation under Tiglath-Pileser, who ascended the throne 745 B.C.[2] The Book of Jonah is a foreign missionary book in the midst of the Old Testament. The predictions of the prophets against the nations otherwise go forth from the prophets' watch-tower in Jerusalem; but Jonah, whose book follows Obadiah's in the canon, is himself sent as " an ambassador among the heathen " (Obad. ver. 1). Even the preaching of Jesus was directed to the circle of the

---

[1] Compare Delitzsch's *Messianic Prophecies*, Edinburgh 1880, p. 59. —C.

[2] See George Rawlinson, *Five Great Monarchies*, London 1871, vol. ii. p. 126.

people of Israel, and in this the apostles were also included before the ascension of the Lord. But here, even in midst of the Old Testament, the barriers to the announcement of salvation are broken down, and with them the barriers of the national exclusiveness.

§ 52. *The Elevation of Prophecy in the Third Epoch.*

After Tiglath-Pileser II. (Phul?[1]), 745–728 B.C., Assyria became a colossus, through which the Israel of the northern kingdom was crushed. Judah likewise, brought to the brink of destruction, is yet rescued under Hezekiah; but it ripens for a like judgment, for the execution of which the Chaldæans are designated. The prophecy of this period, elevated through its all-comprehensive, far-reaching calling, and by the grandeur of its awe-inspiring and glorious character, unfolds the highest beauty of expression. The prophets are intent upon fixing the contents of their discourses in written form; for (1) their prophecies are of universal significance for all ages and nations; (2) the dispersion of Israel through Assyria and Chaldæa is impending; and (3) the time is no longer distant when prophecy itself will be silent. In this epoch, Messianic prophecy also breaks through the night and fire of judgment, more intensely and brightly than ever. Now for the

---

[1] It is still a question whether Tiglath-Pileser and Phul are different names for one individual, or whether they indicate two different persons. Perhaps the former was the sovereign, and the latter his vassal king in Babylon.

first time the Messianic idea is decisively separated
from the present. The image of the Messiah is painted
in the pure ether of the future. It becomes the
treasure of a faith which doubts the present, and
therefore has become so much the more spiritual and
heavenly.

§ 53. *The Judæan Prophet of the Absolute One in the Kingdom of Israel.*

In about the tenth year of Uzziah, that is, in the
twenty-fifth of Jeroboam II., Amos appeared. His
book is dark, but on the outmost edge (ix. 13–15) the
light of promise rises. After he has promised that the
sinful kingdom of Israel shall be sifted among the
nations, but without a single noble grain being lost, he
turns from Israel to Judah, and sees the house of David,
now a falling hut (compare 2 Kings xiv. 13), rising
from its ruins as a divine building, ruling, as in the
former days, over distant nations in the midst of a
richly prospered land, which he describes with the words
of Joel. We have here the reanimation of the Messianic
prophecy (compare Acts xv. 16, where the passage is
cited according to the Septuagint) in the first stadium of
its new progress. Elsewhere in the Book of Amos the
progress of the New Testament in the Old is percep-
tible, especially in the depreciation of animal sacrifice
(Amos v. 21 sqq., compare Acts vii. 42 sq.) and of the
national preference of Israel (ix. 7, compare iii. 1 sq.).

§ 54. *The Ephraimitic Prophet of Love.*

At the end of Amos' activity the beginning of Hosea's is ushered in. The prophecy of Amos flows, as was first remarked by Magnus Friedrich Roos (b. 1727, d. 1803), from the principle of the sovereignty of God the Judge, Hosea's from the principle of the love of God the Compassionate One. The Lamb is indeed still concealed in Jehovah, but in the third chapter the divine side of the promise finds its supplement through the human side. If we compare Hosea iii. 4 sqq. with Amos ix. 11, the restoration of the house of David, and in it of the unity and glory of Israel, is here already brought to a personal expression. Israel wins again what it has lost, and wins it through a second David.

REMARK.—Duhm says[1] that in Amos the religious element is made subservient to the moral, while in Hosea the religious is almost absolutely dominant. The right view is, that Hosea makes love the centre of his idea of God, while Amos makes the power which serves justice the centre. Hosea is, as Ewald (b. 1803, d. 1875) has appropriately characterized him, the prophet of the highly tragical pain of love. It is characteristic that the symbolic representation of the future is mediated in Hosea by means of two marriages. The reason of this is, so to speak, in the erotic character of the prophet.

[1] *Theologie der Propheten*, Bonn 1875, p. 127.

§ 55. *Enrichment of the Knowledge of Redemption under Ahaz.*

The Messianic prophecy of this third epoch attains in Isaiah and his younger contemporary Micah its climax. The sixth year of Hezekiah, in which the northern kingdom was destroyed, is the terminus toward which Messianic prophecy constantly ascends, as represented by the two closely connected prophets. The Isaianic fundamental prophecy concerning Zemach-Jehovah (Isa. iv. 2, which is continued in Jer. xxiii. 5, xxxiii. 15; Zech. iii. 8, vi. 12) is still so held in clare-obscure, and is so enigmatical, that it is questionable whether the sprout of Jehovah is intended personally or as a thing. But after this prophecy, dating from the time of Jotham, there follows in the reign of Ahaz the trilogy of the Messianic prophecies in Isa. vii.–xii. The Son of the virgin whom Isaiah foresees in chapter vii. 14 as not yet born, already lies, according to chapter ix. 5 sq., in the cradle; and in chapter xii. the prophet beholds Him reigning, and describes the righteous, peaceful, and universal sway of this second David, who goes forth from the root of Jesse, that is, out of his stock, from the tree of the Davidic house, which has been deprived of its branches, but which is not without hope, after the forest of Lebanon, representing the world-power, has been cut down.

§ 56. *The Fateful Turning-point of Old Testament History.*

The time of Uzziah, fifty-two years, and of Jotham, sixteen years, was by far the longest period of peace and prosperity in the kingdom since its foundation. But self-confidence, luxury, devotion to heathen customs and modes of worship, were the principal evils of that period, in which Isaiah was called to proclaim the destruction of this false glory. Even towards the end of Jotham's reign, the fulfilment of what had been threatened was prepared. The hostilities of the Syrio-Ephraimitic league began (2 Kings xv. 37). Rezin, the king of Syria, whose capital was Damascus, took possession of the harbour Elath, which Uzziah had conquered from the Edomites (2 Kings xvi. 6; compare xiv. 22). The Judæans who were dwelling there were carried to Damascus (2 Chron. xxviii. 5), and Ahaz was vanquished by Pekah, the king of Israel, in a terribly bloody battle, after which Oded rescued the numerous Judæan captives from the disgrace of slavery (2 Chron. xxviii. 6–15). Both of the armies of the allies, after they had been victorious separately, were now united together, and prepared the main attack against Jerusalem (Isa. vii. 2). In the midst of this danger, Isaiah appears with his son, Shear-jashub, before the king, promises him God's help, and professes his readiness to give every security by an earthly or heavenly sign; but Ahaz declines this, for he has already summoned

the help of Tiglath-Pileser, the king of Assyria. This
is one of the most momentous turning-points in the
history of both Israelitish kingdoms, for the complica-
tion with Assyria effected by Ahaz lays the foundation for the enslavement of Israel through the world-
empire.   It was the time at which Rome was already
founded, the last link in the chain which was to fetter
Israel.[1] Here, on the threshold of the divine judgments, which are executed through the world-empire,
Isaiah raises for the believers the banner of the
Messiah.   The picture which had previously remained
in clare-obscure, growing dim and without any fixed
outline, now becomes a richly coloured painting of a
specific person with a divine essence.

§ 57. *The Separation and Progress of the Image of the
Messiah in Micah.*

Micah in his book, which as it now lies before us
was all written at one time, and was recited in one of
the first years of Hezekiah (Jer. xxv. 18 sq.), before
the fall of Samaria (i. 6), first transposes the type of
David, who attained from the herds (compare the
allusion in iv. 8) and from lowly beginnings to the
fulness of kingly power.   He changes this image into
a definite prophecy, and predicts that the Messiah
will go forth from Bethlehem-Ephratah, at a time
when the house of David will have sunk down to the

---

[1] Compare Delitzsch's *Messianic Prophecies*, Edinburgh 1880, p. 62,
and *supra*, pp. 103, 104.—C.

lowliness of its origin (Micah v. 1). If we leave out of account the controverted prophecies of Isaiah, we shall find even in other respects that Micah in many ways transcends the measure of Isaiah's knowledge. For he not only predicts the Babylonian exile, but also the deliverance from it; and while Isaiah (vii.–xii.) beholds the Messiah together with the Assyrian distresses, and the beginning of His kingdom with the downfall of Assyria, Micah, with far-reaching vision, sees the parousia of the Messiah after the Babylonian exile (Micah iv. v.; compare ii. 12 sq.). He indeed still calls the world-empire by its historical name Assyria (v. 4), or the kingdom of Nimrod (v. 5), yet not Zion and Assyria, but Zion and Babylon are for him opposite poles (vii. 8–10; compare iv. 10).

§ 58. *The Prophecy of the Psalter and of the Book of Proverbs concerning the Son of God.*

With the great prophecies of Isaiah and Micah is associated, as of equal importance, the prophecy of the author of the second psalm [1] concerning God's Royal Son. Here the prophetic expressions concerning the divine personality of the future Christ, and concerning His origin, which extends back to hoary antiquity,[2] are supplemented by the attestation of His Sonship, by

---

[1] Compare Delitzsch's *Messianic Prophecies*, Edinburgh 1880, pp. 69, 70.—C.

[2] The Septuagint version of Micah v. 2, last clause, is : καὶ ἔξοδοι αὐτοῦ ἀπ' ἀρχῆς ἐξ ἡμερῶν αἰῶνος. "And his goings out are from the beginning, from days of the age."

which He has God as His Father, in an extraordinary
way exceeding that of other Davidic kings (2 Sam.
vii. 14). The Old Testament Scriptures contain also
another reference to God's Son (Prov. xxx. 4), an
enigmatic word of the chokma, which has a deeply
significant relation to Psalm ii., when Proverbs viii.
22–31 is taken in connection with it. But this
riddle of Agur [1] was but slightly regarded, while, on
the contrary, the second psalm exercised the most
important influence on the religious knowledge. The
history of the knowledge of salvation is an essential
part of the history of salvation; for what appears in
the New Testament as a fact, prepared the way for
itself in the consciousness of the Old Testament
believers.

§ 59. *Isaiah's Proclamation and his Activity under Hezekiah.*

After Ahaz, who reigned sixteen years, hardened
himself against the word of the prophet, a pause
took place in the prophetic preaching. First in the
year that Ahaz died, Isaiah began to prophesy again
(Isa. xiv. 28); but the prophecies of Isaiah against
the nations (xiii.–xxiii.) are probably transmitted only
in their written form. The Messianic element con-

---

[1] See Ewald's *Biblical Theology*, entitled *Die Lehre der Bibel*,
Göttingen, vol. iii. p. 82. Similar to Agur's enigmatic questions are
the queries in the *Rig-Veda* [compare *Messianic Prophecies*, p. 114].
The questions concern, as Levi Ben-Gerson (Ralbag) says, the causes
of causes, hence the demiurgic powers of nature.

sists solely in indefinite hints at the ideal King
(xvi. 5, xiv. 29), but the prediction of the entrance of
the nations rises all the higher (xviii. 7, xix. 24 sq.).[1]
A picture of Isaiah's public activity is given in his
addresses (xxviii.–xxix., xxxii.), which are throughout
contemporaneous with the first six years of Hezekiah,
and in chapter xxxiii., from the midst of the Assyrian
invasion.[2] We here see that the time of Hezekiah
will restore what Ahaz has destroyed. But even yet
the politics are not theocratic. As Ahaz leaned in
his conflict against Syria - Ephraim on Assyria, so
now it was proposed to shake off the Assyrian yoke
with the help of Egypt. This projected alliance of
the court party was followed by the prophet through
all the stages of its development with annihilating
criticism. In Isa. xxviii. 16 he places another ground
of confidence in opposition to that of the flesh.[3] The
precious corner-stone is the future Son of David, who
even now, with invisible energy, is the unshaken
bearer and Saviour of His people. The reason why
the threatenings of Isaiah against Jerusalem (xxix. 1,
xxxii. 10, 13 sq.) were not fulfilled may be seen from
Jer. xxvi. 17–19, where God is described as repenting
of the evil, which he had determined against Judah, on
account of Hezekiah's prayer.

[1] Compare Delitzsch's *Messianic Prophecies*, pp. 71, 72.—C.

[2] Sennacherib's invasion of Judah happened in one of the last years of
Hezekiah; the four narratives, Isa. xxxvi.–xxxvii. and xxxviii.–xxix.,
are transposed; the date in xxxvi. 1 belonged, as it seems, originally to
the first pair.

[3] Compare Delitzsch's *Messianic Prophecies*, pp. 72, 73.—C.

In chapter xxxiii. reproof and menace are directed against Assyria, because the best of the people, with the king at their head, have turned penitently to Jehovah. In the four narratives contained in Isa. xxxvi.–xxxix., the public activity of Isaiah in the Assyrian period comes to an end. The four narratives stand in unchronological order, for that which is narrated in Isa. xxxviii.–xxxix. precedes chapters xxxvi.–xxxvii. in order of time. The reason for the inversion is that Isaiah in xxxix. 5 sqq., as Merodach-Baladan, the Assyrian vassal king of Babylon, sued for the favour of Hezekiah, foresaw the Babylonian world-dominion, and prophesied the Babylonian exile. The editor of Isaiah has made prediction Isa. xxxix. 6 sqq. the link which binds the two halves of the book together.

REMARK.—The apocalyptic finale (Isa. xxiv.–xxvii.) is a prophetic cycle of the greatest significance for the history of the progress of religious knowledge in the Old Testament. The idea of salvation is here separated from its national externality, and is conceived as radically spiritual and human.

§ 60. *Nahum and Habakkuk.*

Nahum's appearance is connected with the end of Isaiah's and Micah's activity. He beholds in the fall of Assyria the fall of the world-empire in general, and thereafter the restoration of the unity and glory of entire Israel. His standpoint is subsequent to

the Assyrian invasion, which ended with the defeat
of Sennacherib, but before his assassination in the
temple of Nisroch, at the time when Judah had to
fear a terrible revenge from Assyria. At this time
Nahum prophesied the final end of the Assyrian
world-empire, without knowing that the world-empire
would rise against Israel in a new form, but with an
unchanged character. The prophets have the Spirit
"by measure" (John iii. 34). Nahum's range of
vision is limited.

Habakkuk is one of the prophets under Manasseh
(2 Kings xxi. 10–15).[1] What the Old Testament
testifies from the beginning in word and deed, that
only אֱמוּנָה, that is, the firm, abiding, clinging hold on
God's promise and grace, is the only means and way
of life in the midst of death, is pithily expressed by
this prophet in the saying, "The just shall live by
his faith" (Hab. ii. 4, compare Isa. vii. 9, xxviii. 16).
It remains uncertain whether the anointed one (מָשִׁיחַ,
iii. 13) is Josiah or Christ, the ideal King of the
final period. The ground of the prophet's hope is
Jehovah the God of Salvation, the contents of the
vision (Hab. ii. 2) and the object of faith (ii. 4) is,
according to the Septuagint, the Saviour, the Coming
One (Heb. x. 37); but according to its immediate
meaning, the salvation of Jehovah, the vision is per-
sonified, and the thought of a person as its fulfilment
lies near at hand.

[1] Compare the lament in i. 2 with 2 Kings xxi. 16.

§ 61. *The Last Prophecy against Assyria.*

Zephaniah also belongs to the prophets indicated in 2 Kings xxi. 10, who appeared later than Habakkuk, under Josiah, whose father Ammon, during the two years of his reign, and whose grandfather Manasseh, during the fifty years of his reign,[1] had filled the kingdom with all the abominations of a strange idolatry. In the twelfth year (according to 2 Chron. xxxiv. 3) Josiah began to eradicate the idolatry and the local sanctuaries (*bamôth*). In the eighteenth year he completed the reforms in worship to which he was incited by the Tora found in the temple. In the intermediate time between the twelfth and eighteenth years of Josiah, Zephaniah prophesied. He does not name the people whom God uses as the instruments of his punishment; but since judgment falls upon Nineveh, it is the time of its execution by the Chaldæan nation, which he describes as "*Dies iræ, dies illa.*"[2]

Even in chapter ii., where all the surrounding nations are judged, the promise presses in, which concerns the remnant and also includes the nations. In the third chapter reproof and threatening take a new start, but grace succeeds wrath, and iii. 9 forms the turning-point (which is marked with אָז, "then").

---

[1] At the end of his reign Manasseh repented (2 Chron. xxxiii. 13–23), perhaps to his own salvation, but not to the rescue of his people.

[2] This is the beginning of the celebrated judgment hymn of Thomas of Celano. It is taken from Zeph. i. 15.

It is a new pregnant expression which the hope of the future conversion of the heathen takes on : *mutabo populis labium purum.* And in Zeph. iii. 10 the briefest expression is given to that which is prophesied in Isa. lxvi. 18–20, with the combination of Isa. xviii. (compare Zeph. i. 7 with Hab. ii. 20 ; Joel i. 15 ; Isa. xxxiv. 6, xiii. 3). It is the prophecy of the Isaianic type, which is given once more by Zephaniah in a compendium and in a kind of mosaic.

REMARK.—The Assyrian kingdom went down under Asuriddili (Asurdanili), whose reign began in 625 B.C. The year of the catastrophe of Nineveh is at the latest 606 B.C., with which Eusebius nearly agrees, who fixes the fall of Nineveh according to Herodotus in the first year of the forty-third Olympiad, that is, 608 or 607 B.C. The battle of Carchemish occurred in the year 606 or 605 B.C., in which Pharaoh-Necho was defeated by Nebuchadnezzar, the son of Nabopolassar, who died at that time. Nebuchadnezzar therefore hastened from the battle-field to Babylon that he might succeed his father.

§ 62. *Jeremiah's Call and his First Proclamation under Josiah.*

The history of Jeremiah's call in the first chapter of his prophecy is, in all respects, a prognostic of his doing and suffering. He is the prophet to the Gentiles, and we find him in immediate communication with them. In him, as in no other prophet, tenderness and variety of feeling are interpenetrated with great and enduring strength. His calling is directed rather to tearing down than to building up. In this sad office one suffering after another as a confessor befalls him. He represents the martyrdom of the prophets, and probably died as a martyr in Egypt. Kings, princes, priests, and people are constantly arrayed against him; but strong in God, he bids defiance to all their attacks. In the first address (Jer. ii.–iii. 5), the expression "from this time" (מֵעַתָּה, iii. 4 sq.) indicates the religious revolution which entered under Josiah, but which was only of a superficial character. The entire address is like a variation of the first three verses of Isaiah: "I have nourished and brought up children, and they have rebelled against me." Deep pain on account of rejected love is its fundamental feature. In general, the key-note of Jeremiah corresponds to the οὐκ ἠθελήσατε, "Ye would not" (Luke xiii. 34), of the Lord, or His words in Luke xix. 42: "Now they [i.e. the things which belong to thy peace] are hid from thine eyes." The second address (Jer. iii. 6–vi.) dates from the days of Josiah, that is, from a year subsequent to the thirteenth of that king, in which the worship of Jehovah was again restored (Jer. vi. 20). But the prophet, in spite of the glittering restoration, sees to the very bottom of the corruption which is all the while dominant. The next prophecy in order of time (Jer. xxii. 10–12) threatens Shallum, who is also called Jehoahaz (2 Kings xxiii. 30), the son and successor of Josiah, with the fate which was fulfilled by Pharaoh-Necho in

I

sending him as a prisoner to Egypt, where he died
without seeing his native land again.   Instead of
Jehoahaz, Pharaoh-Necho made Eliakim king, whose
name he changed to Jehoiakim (2 Kings xxiii. 34), a
younger son of Josiah ; and the Books of Kings and of
Chronicles describe how he walked in the footsteps of
his godless ancestors, and that in his time the judgment, which since Manasseh had become irreversible,
began to be executed (2 Kings xxiii. 37, xxiv. 2-4).
We see from Jer. xx. 23-26 that he, like Manasseh,
was a murderer of the prophets.

§ 63.   *Jeremiah's Activity until the Catastrophe.*

In the defeat of the Egyptians in the fourth year of
Jehoiakim, Jeremiah recognised the true commencement of the Chaldæan judgment on the nations which
is now beginning.   Looking back upon the twenty-
three years of his fruitless activity, he announces (xxv.)
a servitude of seventy years, which is to be followed
by the fall of the Chaldæan empire (compare Dan. ix. 2).
The " wine-cup of this fury " finally comes to the king
Sheshach, which is an enigmatic name for Babylon
(Jer. xxv. 26, li. 41), the instrument itself of punitive
judgment.   The book, in the form of a roll, containing
the addresses of the prophet until the fourth year of
Jehoiakim, which had been written down by Baruch
after the dictation of the prophet, was brought at the
command of the king, and was finally burned by him
(Jer. xxxvi., xlv.).   Jehoiakim was succeeded by his

son Jehoiachin when he was eighteen years of age
(2 Kings xxiv. 8, compare 2 Chron. xxxvi. 9). Against
him the prophecy (Jer. xxii. 20-30) was directed
which deprived the Solomonic line of the throne for
all the future. The Babylonian exile began with
Jehoiachin. The carrying away to Babylon, after a
reign of three months, in 596 B.C., is the era of Ezekiel.
In contradiction to the false prophets of the exile,
Jeremiah now prophesied in his letter to the captives
(xxix. 1–23) that the Judæan state must be completely destroyed. Under Zedekiah, Josiah's youngest
son, whom Nebuchadnezzar had put in Jehoiachin's
place, and who, in the ninth year of his reign, revolted
against Babylon, Jeremiah continued to demand
submission to the Chaldæan power with terrible per-
sistency, and to threaten destruction in case of continued
opposition (Jer. xxvii., xxviii., xxi. 1–10, xxxiv.).
Jerusalem was now besieged by the Chaldæans, but
they were forced by Pharaoh-Hophra to raise the siege.
Jeremiah, however, foretold their return, and continued
to threaten the worst (Jer. xxxvii. 3–10). He was
considered by those who had a controlling voice as a
traitor to his fatherland. They let him down into a
miry cistern, from which he was freed by Ebed-melech
the Cushite, not without the approval of the unfortunate and not ignoble, though weak king. On the
ninth of Tammuz (July) of the eleventh year of Zedekiah, Jerusalem became a prey to the Chaldæans after
a siege of eighteen months. Jeremiah was compelled
to wander in fetters with the other exiles to Ramah.

There, by the command of Nebuchadnezzar, he was left
free to choose whether he would remain in the land or
go to Babylon. He preferred the former, and betook
himself to Gedaliah (xxxix., xl. 1–6). This favourable
treatment of Jeremiah was a reward which seemed to
confirm the opinion of those who considered him an
enemy of his fatherland; yet he was a patriot, who did
not care for the favour or displeasure of men. He
loved his people, but he did not flatter them; and he
announced God's will, which was made known to him,
although it was opposed to his own wishes and feelings.
A glance at the conflict within him is afforded by
vi. 11, xv. 17 sqq. Isaiah and Ezekiel, like Jeremiah,
express their moral condemnation of the breach of the
oath on the part of the Jewish vassal kings.[1]

§ 64. *The Progress in the Recognition of Redemption by Jeremiah.*

It is evident that the New Testament period is
drawing ever nearer, from the fact that as in general
Jeremiah makes the covenant, as a religious relation,
the centre of his prophecy, so he comprehends the
prophecy of a future renewal of it in the idea, and in

[1] Isaiah reproaches Hezekiah for his revolt from Sennacherib, the
great king of Assyria, in which he leans upon Egypt (compare
Isa. xxviii. 15). In the same way Ezekiel reproaches Zedekiah for
his revolt from the great king of Babylon, xvii. 15 : "But he rebelled
against him in sending his ambassadors into Egypt, that they might
give him horses and much people. Shall he prosper? shall he escape
that doeth such things? or shall he break the covenant and be delivered?"

the designation, of "a new covenant" (Jer. xxxi. 31).
Another mark of progress is in this, that Jeremiah
gives personality its rights, and places it beyond the
consequences of family connection, in which the
personality, according to the dominant doctrine of
retribution, had disappeared (xxxi. 29 sq.). This is
the same theme of which Ezekiel treats more particularly in a similar spirit (xviii., xxxiii.). Hence
the old covenant is not only a relation of God to
His people, but also to each individual as a person.
From the time of the new covenant, the law of God
becomes a living spirit, and is no longer a dead letter;
it is henceforth an inward possession and inclination,
and the recognition of God and His salvation is not
confined to a body of teachers, but becomes the
common possession of all (Jer. xxxi. 31–34). A
third advance is the designation of the Messiah, the
second David, as the "Righteous Sprout" (Jer. xxiii.
5; after 2 Sam. xxiii. 4; Isa. iv. 2), and as "Jehovah
our Righteousness" (Jer. xxiii. 5), the One in whom
Jehovah dwells as His people's righteousness, that is,
as "the just and the justifier" (Rom. iii. 26), in the
same way that He dwells in Jerusalem (xxxiii. 14–
16); the Messiah is therefore like the temple of God,
who is at the same time gracious and just. The
person of the Messiah is here understood ethically,
and the redemption inwardly, and a "righteousness of
God" (Rom. i. 17), mediated through the second
David, as its chief fruit. The consolatory book of
Jeremiah, comprising chapters xxx. and xxxi., which

should be held to have been revealed at Ramah,
according to the transposed superscription[1] (Jer. xl. 1),
forms a companion-piece to Isa. xl.–lxvi. The tone
of Jer. xxx. 8–10, compare xlvi. 27 sq., is entirely
Deutero-Isaianic.

§ 65. *The Progress in the Recognition of Redemption by Ezekiel.*

Ezekiel worked in Babylon contemporaneously with
Jeremiah, who remained in Judæa until after Gedaliah's
assassination, when he was torn away by the emigrants
into Egypt (Jer. xl. 7–xliii. 7). Jeremiah stood with
the exiles of Babylon in lively communication, but he
himself never went thither. Ezekiel is one of the
ten thousand who, in the third month of the reign of
Jehoiachin, 596 B.C., were transplanted to the Chaldæan
country, where for more than twenty years he dwelt
in Tel-Abib, a place on the Chebâr, one of the branches
or canals of the Euphrates, among the exiles, whose
elders assembled with him (Ezek. viii. 1, xiv. 1,
xx. 3). He is the greatest beholder of visions among
the prophets. His vision of the Mercaba, that is, of
the divine chariot (Ezek. i.–iii., viii.–xi.), is the
grandest of all Biblical visions. It is the throne of
Jehovah above the cherubim of the earthly holy of
holies, which here becomes a living antitype to the
prophet. Upon the wonderful pedestal, in the shape

---

[1] Compare Delitzsch's *Messianic Prophecies*, Edinburgh 1880, § 50,
p. 79.—C.

of a wagon formed of four living animals, which have
a manifold but predominantly human form, and of
the living wheels, which are covered over and over
with eyes, he sees a throne of sapphire, and upon the
throne a form " like the appearance of a man," clothed
from his loins upward in the brightness of fire as of
gleaming brass, and from his loins downward in the
milder hues of the rainbow.   Here Jehovah appears
for the first time in an entirely human manner; the
One who as lawgiver had forbidden that a human
likeness should be made of Him (Ex. xx. 4; Deut.
iv. 15–18), now represents Himself in human form;
for the time of the incarnation is now drawing nearer,
therefore Israel must be accustomed to think of God
in a human way, after the better part of the nation
has been weaned, by means of the exile, from thinking
of him as human in a heathen manner.   The driver
of the chariot appears in human form, and causes the
cherubim to destroy the temple at Jerusalem in order
to build another, and to fill it with His presence.

§ 66. *Ezekiel's Portrait of the Messiah.*

The Book of Ezekiel contains relatively many prophecies concerning the Messiah, and everywhere the
present is the dark foil of the Messiah's picture.   It
is formed according to the law of contrast.   The second
David is the counterpart of the wicked shepherds of
Israel.   He here appears in an ethical activity, like
the good Shepherd who seeks that which was lost

(Ezek. xxxiv. 16, 23 sq.; compare xxxvii. 24), and in
such a unique pre-eminent relation to God, that it is
impossible to identify with him the prince of the
eschatological state of the twelve tribes (Ezek. xl.–
xlviii.).   Even Jeremiah affords a prospect of holy,
glorious princes who have a right to the priestly
office (Jer. xxx. 21; compare xxxiii. 17 and 21); yet
the second David is not one of them, but towers above
them all (Jer. xxx. 9).   He is, according to Ezek.
xvii. 22, the tender twig of cedar which, planted upon
a lofty mountain, becomes a tree giving shade to the
world (compare Isa. xi. 1 and liii. 2).   He is, according
to Ezek. xxi. 32 [1] (E.V. ver. 27), the One whose is
the kingdom (שֶׁלֹּה, *is cujus est regnum*), the *Shellōh*, at
whom the benediction upon Judah (Gen. xlix. 10)
is aimed.

§ 67. *The Four Types among the Prophets.*

The significance of the two great prophets for the
redemptive history is not limited to their prophecies.
It consists in their entire activity, which prepares the
foundation for the coming of the second David; and
since the Spirit of God is in them, their fortunes form
the prelude of His.   Isaiah, with his preaching, which
decides the rejection of the mass of Israel (Matt. xiii.
13–15; John xii. 37–41; Acts xxviii. 25–27; Rom.
xi. 7 sq.), and with the *ecclesia in ecclesia*, that is, the
little flock (Luke xii. 32), around him, is a type of

---

[1] Compare Delitzsch's *Messianic Prophecies*, pp. 34, 35.—C.

Jesus (Heb. ii. 13), who is set for the fall and rising
again of many, and of the spiritual children who are
gathered about Him, and to whom the kingdom is
assigned.   Jeremiah's typical character is of an entirely
different kind.   As Elijah represents the conflict and
Elisha the triumph of prophetism, so Isaiah represents
the power of the prophets in acting, and Jeremiah
their strength in suffering.   He is the afflicted priestly
prophet, as David is the suffering king.   Hence the
passion psalms of David, and the lamentation of Job,
and the Deutero-Isaianic passional, are re-echoed from
his mouth.   He is not the Servant of Jehovah
described in Isa. liii., but he and David prefigure Him
most strikingly.

§ 68. *Jeremiah and Ezekiel as Prophets of the Catastrophe.*

It was the vocation of the priestly pair of prophets
to accompany the kingdom of Judah on its final course
to destruction with their announcement of wrath and
comfort.   Their vocation is similar to that of Hosea
for the kingdom of Israel.   Isaiah was able to deliver
his people once more from destruction in the Assyrian
troubles (Sirach xlviii. 20; compare 2 Chron. xxxii. 20).
But the prayers of Jeremiah and Ezekiel rebound, and
in a fearful gradation intercession is forbidden them,
and its uselessness is ever clearer (Jer. vii. 16, xi.
14, xiv. 11 sq., xv. 1 ; Ezek. xii. 20).   Ezekiel
beholds how God's presence deserts the temple, and

fire from between the cherubim is made ready to be scattered upon Jerusalem. Images of that which is most dreadful are set before him, and he becomes at the command of Jehovah the pliant model through which He represents the most terrible things in the future. Jeremiah contends against the disloyal Egyptian politics of the court party, and against the demagogic deceptions of the false prophets. He still seeks, even in the last days, to protect His people from the worst, by dissuasion from a desperate struggle. Yet he does not rescue Jerusalem, but only himself to see its ruins consume in smoke,—a sight which wastes his flesh and breaks his bones (Lam. iii. 4). The illness of the kingdom of Judah is unto death. Hence Aholibah behaved like Aholah, and comes to a like end (Ezek. xxiii.). This fifth period changes in this, that the beasts which had gone up from the sea of nations devour Judah as well as Israel. The entire people, which was divided since Rehoboam in their own land, is now gathered outside of their country in the heathen world; but prophecy, like the soul after it has fled from the body, hovers over the *disjecta membra* as a pledge of Israel's resurrection.

SIXTH PERIOD.

FROM THE EXILE UNTIL THE APPEARANCE OF JESUS CHRIST. THE FIRST HALF OF THIS PERIOD IS CHARACTERIZED BY THE DAWNING RECOGNITION OF THE MEDIATOR AND THE LOGOS.

§ 69. *The Characteristics of this Period.*

A S on the sixth day of the hexahemeron the organic creation in its progressive individualization finally attained its goal in the person of man created in God's image, so the essential part of this sixth period is that out of the corrupted mass (*massa perdita*) of entire Israel a congregation is separated, which is in truth Jehovah's flock (Ps. lxviii. 5) and "turtle-dove" (Ps. lxxiv. 19), and whose typical peculiarity is completed in the man who is unique in his personality and in his likeness to God. There has always been indeed a congregation of Jehovah; but its breach with fleshly Israel now becomes deeper, its solidarity with the people as such looser, its calling in the present more important, and its significance for the future greater than ever. The Church of Jehovah now emerges in a less mixed, less confined, but more spiritual form. Wellhausen makes a fundamental mistake when he affirms that the post-exilic priestly codex first set the congregation (קָהָל or עֵדָה) in the place of the people. The subject of the worship was from the very beginning the congregation of the people, to which Israel through the Sinaitic legislation was raised, and the New Testament Church is not the continuation of this national congregation, but its transformation into a spiritual congregation, whose members are not only united through flesh and blood, but also through the bond of the new birth. It is true that in proportion as the people in the exile were deprived of the unity of the fatherland and the unity of the state, the religious unity occupied the foreground, but still only upon a national basis. In the New Testament Church, on the contrary, the national element is removed—in Christ there is neither Greek nor Jew, but Christ is all and in all (Col. iii. 11).

§ 70. *The Significance of the Exile for the Redemptive History.*

It is the natural course of the divine wisdom in the tutorial progress of revelation, that everything new which is to be developed must first lie enveloped in temporary embryogenic coverings. This progress is from limitation to non-limitation, from the state of the chrysalis to the breaking through of the *psyche*, from particularism to *universalism*, from guardianship and childhood to freedom and majority. So the Israel of the exile is removed from its local boundaries, and is loosed from its political community; its unity is almost exclusively reduced to the unity of faith and confession, for the sojourn "outside of the Holy Land" occasioned a partial suspension of the law.   Israel was in the exile not only without a king, but also without a sacrifice (Hos. iii. 4).   And yet, so far as their God now took the place of the temple (Ezek. xi. 16), they attained something higher than ever before.   They were placed in the midst of the execution of their world-wide calling, and found themselves in a preparatory school for the New Testament worship of God in spirit and in truth.

§ 71. *The Servant of Jehovah among the Exiles.*

The mass of the people of Israel fell into heathenism.   The Book of Ezekiel shows how the Babylonian exiles sought to unite the service of idols and that of Jehovah, and adopted the idolatrous worship of the Chaldæans as old Israel did that of the Egyptians (Ezek. xx. and elsewhere).   Still deeper views into the circumstances of the exile are afforded by Isa. xl.–lxvi. The national consciousness and the love of their countrymen were almost extinguished in the majority of the exiles.   The younger generation pursued the same course as the older one which had occasioned the exile.   But there were also those who did not follow their own way, but the way of Jehovah, and mourned for Zion.   They were hated and persecuted. Their heathen brethren made common cause with

their Babylonian oppressors.   Under the form of a
servant, and the misery of the deepest humiliation, this
true congregation of Jehovah carried the salvation of
their people and of the heathen on their hearts.   The
conception of the Servant of Jehovah in Isa. xl.–lxvi.,
with respect to its lowest broad basis, is entire Israel;
with respect to its centre it is the congregation remaining true to God, which in the midst of the
dispersion is the scattered seed of the future congregation growing together from Israel and the heathen.
From this centre the conception becomes personal.
Its pyramidal apex is the future Christ, in whom the
sufferings of the congregation of Jehovah are reproduced and culminate, and by whom Israel's redemptive calling is completed.[1]

§ 72. *The Idea of the Servant of Jehovah as the Con-centration of hitherto scattered Elements.*

All forms of the previous prefiguration of salvation
are united in the conception of the Servant of Jehovah.

(1) The consolatory book (Isa. xl.–lxvi.) begins at
once with the announcement that all flesh shall see
the unveiled glory of Jehovah, of God the Redeemer
(Isa. xl. 5, compare lix. 20 ; Matt. iii. 3 ; Rom. xi. 26).
The name Jehovah is at the very point of giving birth
to the name Jesus (Isa. lxii. 11, xlix. 6).

(2) The Servant of Jehovah is the One in whom
the sure mercies of David are fulfilled (Isa. lv. 3).

---

[1] Compare *Messianic Prophecies*, pp. 84, 85.

He is the Seed of Abraham (Isa. xli. 8); nay, the
prophecy concerning Him has a background reaching
to the seed of the woman in the protevangelium
(Isa. xlix. 1,[1] compare the reference to the serpent,
lxv. 25).

(3) He is a prophet (Isa. xlii. 4); He is a priest,
for He offers Himself and atones for sins (Isa. liii.).
He is King, for all kings do Him homage (Isa. lii. 15).
The Deuteronomic prophecy concerning the great
Prophet, the Messianic prophecy since Balaam, and
the prophecy of David concerning a King after the
order of Melchizedek, here find a living embodiment.

(4) He takes the burden of the guilt of His people
upon His heart and conscience, and God allows Him
to suffer and die for them, that in Him, the Beloved,
He may make His people a justified and sanctified
congregation. The riddle of the accommodated permission of animal sacrifice, and the connection of the
atonement (כַּפָּרָה) with the blood, finds its explanation
here in the depths of the divine decree of salvation
(Isa. liii. 6, 10); and the longing look of the Israel of
the exile back to the sacrificial worship, is here
directed to the One who is the truth and end of all
sacrifice. The Psalms and Prophets have until now
symbolically depreciated the value of the sacrificial
worship, without explaining it typically. Here first
in Isa. xl.–lxvi. the type of the sacrificial blood, which
was previously dumb, begins to speak.

[1] Professor Delitzsch considers it significant that no mention is made
of a father in this passage.—C.

§ 73. *The Idea of the Servant of Jehovah as a new Source of Knowledge.*

The one-sided Messianic image of the king, which previously had only been supplemented by the type of David, is now removed. The Servant of Jehovah ascends through death and the grave to glory (*status duplex*[1]). The connecting line is drawn between the prophet, the king, and the priest of the future. The Servant of Jehovah is all three at the same time (*munus triplex*), and after the idea of the Messiah is merged in the conception of Israel as the Servant of Jehovah, there arises, since the Messianic idea re-ascends personally from this national basis, a new, deeper, and so to speak, more organic relation of the Future One to Israel (*unio mystica*). He is called Israel,[2] because Israel's being is concentrated in Him, like the union of the separate rays of light in the sun. The Church is His body, and He is its head. In addition to this, the redemption is chiefly considered as a redemption from sin, and the substance of the redemption is understood as an atonement and as a reconciliation, but principally as a reconciliation of the divine justice with the divine love. Jehovah causes the storm of His wrath to go over His Servant, who brings Himself to Him as a trespass-offering (אָשָׁם), that is, as a vicarious satis-

---

[1] *Status exinanitionis* and *status exaltationis.*

[2] Isa. xlix. 3: "Thou art my servant, O Israel, in whom I will be glorified."

faction,[1] that He may prepare a free way for His love.

§ 74. *Ezekiel's New Tora.*

We now contrast Ezekiel's prophecies concerning the last things with Isa. xl.–lxvi., which is more like a New Testament than an Old Testament book. The closing chapters of Ezekiel (xl.–xlviii.) seem to stand in glaring contradiction to everything of a New Testament character, such as we rejoice to find in Deutero-Isaiah. As in the New Testament Apocalypse the Church, which during the tribulations from Antichrist is blended together, and again made complete through the first resurrection, still has to endure a final storm from the heathen world; so there follows in Ezekiel, upon the great vision of the reawakening and restoration of Israel as a reunited people (Ezek. xxxvii.), the prediction of the march of Gog against the people of God, and the destruction of the army of this northern people, in which world-power and world-hatred finally close on each other. This prediction is immediately connected with the great tableau of the new worship of God, and of the new religious and political state of entire Israel. It is the post-exilic, final period, in which the prophet sees, in a vision, a new temple outside of the circuit of the city, and a land equally divided in oblong parts among the twelve tribes, and

---

[1] The idea of the sin-offering is that of expiation, and the idea of the trespass-offering is that of satisfaction, that is, a covering of a debt, which is considered as guilt, by an equivalent.

K

a new Jerusalem inhabited by citizens of all the tribes, as the capital of the people now dwelling exclusively on this side Jordan. These nine chapters form one of the greatest Biblical riddles. The Synagogue is here helpless, for the new order of things stands in the sharpest contradiction to all parts of the Mosaic law. And the Church is involved in embarrassment through the prospective renewal of the sacrificial worship. The allegorical method of interpretation affords no help. It cannot even be carried through in respect to the fountain which flows from the threshold of the east door of the temple (Ezek. xlvii. 1–12).

REMARK.—The closing chapters of the Book of Ezekiel (xl.–xlviii.), according to the latest theory of the Pentateuch, furnish the real key to the history of its origin, and especially to its final stadia. The Tora of Ezekiel is regarded as a transition to the legislation of the Elohistic Tora; and since this is the foundation of Jewish legalism,[1] Smend [2] assigns to the prophet Ezekiel the doubtful honour of being the father of Judaism. Nevertheless we still consider it as certain that the Elohistic Tora is older than that of Ezekiel,[3] and that the Tora of Ezekiel stands in a dependent relation to the Elohistic Tora, simplifying and remodelling its contents. Thus, for example, in the holy place (*sanctum*) of Ezekiel's temple there is

[1] See chapter i. on *Nomismus*, in Weber's *System der Altsynagogalen Palaestinischen Theologie*, Leipzig 1880.

[2] *Der Prophet Ezechiel*, Leipzig 1880.

[3] Compare Delitzsch, *Pentateuch-Kritische Studien*, in Luthardt's *Zeitschrift*, Leipzig 1880, pp. 279–290.

no candle, and no table of shew-bread, but instead of the golden altar of incense, only a simple wooden table (Ezek. xli. 22), that is, an altar; for as Ezekiel here calls the altar of incense a table, so in xliv. 16, like Malachi (i. 7), he designates the altar of burnt-offering as a table. The removal of all non-Israelites from the external service of the sanctuary, the abolition of the high-priesthood, the regulations concerning the position of the prince as such, and as the leading member of the Church,—all this and much more is to be explained by the antagonism in which the new order of things stands to the unforgotten abuses and corruptions of the past.

§ 75. *The true Significance of Ezekiel's Republic.*

What shall we say then? Is Ezekiel a dreamer, and is his picture a Utopia? No, it is a prophecy, but one which has remained unfulfilled, and which, in its present form, never will be fulfilled, because the development of the history of salvation has run past the fulfilment. The fulfilment is connected with a condition[1] which did not take place after the expiration of the exile. The prophet beholds the final period and the end of the exile, according to the law of perspective[2] together. The Israelitic community, in its

[1] Ezek. xliii. 10 sq.: "Thou Son of man, show the house to the house of Israel, that they may be ashamed of their iniquities; and let them measure the plan, and if they be ashamed of all that they have done, show them the form of the house," etc.

[2] The following quotations from C. A. Crusius (b. 1715, d. 1775), and Bengel (b. 1687, d. 1752), as given by Delitzsch, *Die biblisch pro-*

ecclesiastical and civil character, takes on a form for Ezekiel after the exile, as here described, under the condition and presupposition that the Israel of both kingdoms will return from foreign lands with a renewal of their first love.　But since this did not take place, this great prediction is overtaken by the history of the fulfilment, which, instead of the stone temple, has placed the spiritual temple of the Church as the body whose head is Christ.　It is characteristic of this picture that the second David has no place in it.　Hence it is only relatively eschatological and more ceremonial, external and peripheral, than evangelical, spiritual, and central.　Nevertheless it is an important link in the chain of prophecy which prepares the way for the New Testament, because—

(1) It is a testimony in the midst of the Old Testament against the unchangeable cháracter of the Tora, and, so to speak, a shattering of its stone letter.

(2) It is a step forward from the variegated character and splendour of the Old Testament worship to the New Testament worship of God in spirit and in truth.

phetische Theologie, etc., Berlin 1845, p. 99 sq., may serve to illustrate what is intended by the law of perspective : " The prophets behold the future, by means of the light of divine illumination, as we do the sidereal heavens.　To us the stars appear as if they were on one level ; we do not distinguish their distance from us, and from one another."— Crusius.　Compare a part of Bengel's comment on Matt. xxiv. 29 : " *Prophetia est, ut pictura regionis cujuspiam, quæ in proximo tecta et calles et pontes notat distincte ; procul, valles et montes latissime patentes in augustias cogit.*"　" Prophecy is like a picture of a certain region, which indicates the houses, paths, and bridges near at hand distinctly, but compresses the valleys and mountains extending very far away into a narrow compass."

§ 76. *Transition of the World-Empire to the Persians.*

The deliverance prophesied by Jeremiah, Deutero-Isaiah, and Ezekiel, from the Assyrio-Babylonian servitude and exile, was prepared by the fall of Nineveh, and subsequently by that of Babylon. After Cyaxares and Nebuchadnezzar had conquered Nineveh, and so had made an end of the Assyrian empire (606 B.C.), there existed for a time by the side of the Babylonian a not less powerful Median empire; and this became through Cyrus, who was from the Persian family of the Achæmenidæ, and who dethroned Astyages the Mede (549 B.C.), a Persian empire which had dominion from the Hindoo Koosh Mountains to the Ægean Sea, and even over Egypt. The fall of Babylon (538 B.C.) under its last ruler Nabonid, whose son was Belshazzar, as is attested by inscriptions, became the deliverance of Israel from its imprisonment. Cyrus gave the exiles their freedom (537 B.C.), of whom at first about one hundred and fifty thousand from the tribes of Judah and Benjamin, and who were to a large extent of Levitical and priestly extraction, returned home under the leadership of the prince Zerubbabel, and of the high priest Joshua, with the permission to rebuild the temple.

§ 77. *The Contrast between the Period of Restoration and the Prophet's Vision.*

When, after the first year of Cyrus' monarchy (537 B.C.), a part of the people reassembled upon domestic soil, it soon appeared that prophecy was not only divine, but human.   Both the expansion of the prophet's vision, which is wrought by the Holy Spirit, as well as the natural limitation of his vision, which the Spirit does not remove, serve the divine plan of redemption ; for if prophecy had possessed and afforded a definite chronological knowledge concerning the course of the future, it would have cut off all desire to press toward the goal of the offered prize. It is therefore precisely what we might expect, that the prophets of the exile behold the consummation of all things in close connection with the end of the exile, and that those who return hope to experience this consummation, or something of it.   Hence such psalms as cxviii. are full of exultation, of glory, and of triumph.   But when, in the second year of the return, the foundation of the new temple was laid (534 B.C.), there was mingled with the shout of joy loud weeping on account of the miserable beginning (Ezra iii. 12) ; and as even under Cyrus, until Pseudo-Smerdis, the building of the temple was discontinued, the people were still caused to feel all the while their servile dependence.

§ 78. *The Progress in the Building of the Temple under the Co-operation of the Prophets.*

The preparation for the building prospered in the second year of the return until the laying of the foundation, but the Samaritans induced Cyrus to put a stop to the enterprise; and this hindrance continued under Cambyses (529–522 B.C.) and the usurper Pseudo-Smerdis (522–521 B.C.). But in the second year of Darius Hystaspis (520 B.C.), the prophets Haggai and Zechariah succeeded in inciting the people and their officers to the resumption of the building. At this time the undertaking was not only allowed, but was also favoured from Ecbatana. When Malachi appeared, the temple had long since been completed (516 B.C.), namely in the sixth year of Darius, on the third of Adar, or March (Ezra vi. 15). The friendly feeling of the Achæmenidæan rulers still continued. In the seventh year of Artaxerxes I. Longimanus (465–424 B.C.), Ezra came with a new company of exiles to Jerusalem (458 B.C.); and as Ezra the scribe, so Nehemiah the provincial governor (*tirshata*) laboured for the restoration of the Jewish community upon the basis of the Mosaic Tora. As Ezra read the Tora in the year 444 B.C., Nehemiah was present (Neh. viii. 1–12), who in the twentieth year of Artaxerxes (445 B.C.) had come to Jerusalem while it was still lying in ruins, and first after twelve years of public service returned to the court of Artaxerxes (433 B.C.). Malachi's activity, in a similar reformatory spirit, falls at the time when Nehemiah had returned to the Persian court. He is one of the prophets whose relation to Nehemiah (Neh. vi. 7) was calumniously misrepresented. Nehemiah returned once more to Jerusalem (comp. Neh. xiii. 6); but we cannot determine from this passage whether his return was under

Artaxerxes or under Darius II. Nothus, who reigned from 423 to 404 B.C. The immorality of the mixed marriages (Ezra ix., x.) had already gained ground (Neh. xiii. 23), and, moreover, a heathen rabble had found quarters among the Jewish people (Neh. xiii. 1–3, compare Deut. xxiii. 4–6).

REMARK.—Since Joel presupposes the legal exist-ence of the worship in the central sanctuary at Jeru-salem, he is brought down by the adherents of the Reuss-Graf theory of the Pentateuch to the post-exilic period. Merx[1] holds that he is to be assigned to the time after the accomplishment of Nehemiah's reform, and that he represents the transition from the pro-phets to the scribes. Stade, in his *University Pro-gramme*,[2] concludes that Joel belongs to a late age because he mentions the Ionians. But Obadiah, Joel, and Amos, in their relation to the unfortunate event under Joram which became the real beginning of a Jewish exile (*galuth*), form an inseparable trilogy.

§ 79. *Daniel, the Confessor and Seer.*

Daniel and his three friends, concerning whom a narrative is found in the book which bears his name, belong to the servants of Jehovah who mourned in the exile for Zion, and were ready to seal their faith with their blood. The Book of Daniel is divided into narratives (i.–vi.) and visions (vii.–xii.). The

---

[1] *Die Prophetie des Joel*, Halle 1879.
[2] *De populo Javan*, Giessen 1880.

historical character of his person is attested by Ezekiel, who mentions him as pre-eminent for his righteousness (xiv. 14, 20), and for his wisdom in regard to mysteries (xxviii. 3). As Isaiah xl.–lxvi. is a consolatory book for the Babylonian exiles, so the Book of Daniel is a book of consolation for the confessors and martyrs of the time of the Seleucidæ. This book which bears his name does not indicate that it was written by him. But nothing prevents us from supposing that there were traditional Babylonio-Persian narratives and traditional prophecies of Daniel, which the author of the book has digested in order to strengthen his contemporaries in their faith through instructive examples and comforting prospects. The visions of Daniel, since he stands over against heathen astrologers and magicians, are of such a kind as his personality would lead us to expect. Nor should we be surprised, in view of his surroundings, that his prophecies have a mantic[1] character, and that his words correspond in their horizon and their political significance to his honourable position as a statesman, and to the universal range of vision which he thereby enjoyed. He can only be compared with Balaam, whose last words (Num. xxiv. 23 sq.) correspond to the horizon of the Book of Daniel; for the ships of Chittim,[2] through which the Roman world-dominion is announced, are also the farthest point of Daniel's perspective, which extends until the appear-

---

[1] Compare Delitzsch's *Messianic Prophecies*, pp. 17–20, 23.
[2] See *ibid*. p. 41, Rem. 1.

ance of the Roman fleet before Alexandria with the
ambassador Caius Popilius Lænas, who compelled
Antiochus to leave Egypt and to restore Ptolemæus
Philometor (168 B.C.). But weighty reasons are
favourable to the composition of the Danielian apocalypse, as we now have it, about the year 170 B.C.,
and hence it is one of the latest books in the Old
Testament. Its narrative portion is advantageously
contrasted with the Book of Esther. It cannot be
regarded as ceremonial narrowness that Daniel and
his friends observed the laws of the Tora concerning
food (Dan. i.). But besides, he was, with his friends,
a model of heroic faith, and knew how to combine
fidelity in the service of his human master with
fidelity to the true God. The last date of his history
is the third year of Cyrus, probably the year in which,
through the intrigues of the Samaritans, the building
of the temple ceased. We shall return later to the
visions of the book, and only affirm here that Daniel
in his doing and suffering is a worthy representative
of those servants of Jehovah whom Deutero-Isaiah
renders conspicuous above the mass, as the kernel of
Israel, and as the heirs of salvation.

§ 80. *The Conclusion of Prophecy.*

It is evident from Isa. xl.–lxvi., more than from
Jeremiah and Ezekiel, what a mighty revolution the
exile was intended to produce in Israel's view of

itself and in the Messianic hope. Israel is thereafter
in a position to know that it is not to conquer the
world with iron, but with spiritual weapons. Haggai
comprehends the blessing of the Messianic age in the
one word " peace " (שָׁלוֹם). Israel, which in a strange
land became a congregation of confessors and martyrs,
can now recognise that the way of the congregation of
Jehovah, which forms the kernel of the mass, passes
through tribulation to glory, and that therefore the
way of the Mediator of salvation, in whom Israel's
history is recapitulated and culminates, can be none
other. Zechariah continues the great passional, Isa.
lii. 13–liii. The Messiah dies, slain by His own
people, who in the last days penitently desire to
return to Him whom they have ignominiously ignored.[1]
Israel now knows that in order to become perfect it
needs a fresh manifestation of the divine presence in
its midst, as in the days of the Mosaic legislation.
Malachi prophesies the parousia of the Lord Himself,
who comes to His temple. He comes in His
messenger, the angel of the covenant, in whom the
angelophanies, since Gen. xv., have been fulfilled. The
spiritual glory of the king, the human form, the unity
of Godhead and humanity, attain in these three post-
exilic prophets an expression which terminates the
development of the Messianic hope.

REMARK 1. — Subsequently to the Assyrio-Babylonian exile, Israel never again, for any great length
of time, became a completely independent and politi-

---

[1] Compare Delitzsch's *Messianic Prophecies*, p. 104 sqq.

cally united nation, but remained in subjection to the kingdoms of this world. Its masters have only changed their names. From this servitude it was designed to develop the knowledge in Israel that its true greatness was not political, but spiritual.

REMARK 2.——Subsequently to the exile it became clearer than ever, that not the entire people of the law and of the circumcision as such is God's people, but a congregation within the entire people, which is persecuted by the Israelitic as well as the heathen world unto blood. It followed from this, that if a mediator of redemption was to arise out of Israel, he would share the form of a servant of the persecuted Church (*ecclesia pressa*), and would ascend through suffering to glory.

REMARK 3.——Subsequently to the exile, Israel must know that human help is of no avail, and that no man has provided the longed-for redemption. God Himself must redeem them a second time, as in the days of the deliverance out of Egypt. The *angelophanies* of the primitive period must attain their goal in a humanly mediated theophany.

§ 81. *The Judaism of the Book of Esther.*

Between the sixth year of Darius (516 B.C.), the year of the completion of the temple, and the seventh year of Artaxerxes I. Longimanus (458 B.C.), the year of the arrival of Ezra and his train, falls the reign of

Xerxes (485-465 B.C.).   During his reign the history
of the Book of Esther seems to have taken place,
which is designed to explain and glorify the Purim
festival.   Since this book has throughout a Persian
stamp, without the least trace of Grecian influence,
whatever one may think about its historical character,
it is certainly a mirror of the form of Judaism among
the dispersion of the second half of the Persian period.
The edict secured by Haman, which ordered that all
the Jews of the Persian empire should be destroyed
on the thirteenth of Adar (March), had to yield to an
edict obtained by Esther and Mordecai, which gave
the Jews the liberty on the same day to gather
together for the preservation of their lives, to destroy
their enemies, and to plunder their possessions.   On
the thirteenth of Adar the massacre began, in which
the Jews were assisted by the royal officers.   In
Susa alone they killed five hundred men, besides the
ten sons of Haman ; but they did not take any plunder.
On Esther's petition, the concession granted to her
countrymen is extended to the fourteenth of Adar,
at which time three hundred men fell again in Susa.
The book reckons those that fell in the provinces outside of Susa at seventy-five thousand.   Hence the
hunting down of the Jews planned by Haman was
revenged through the same bloodthirsty treatment of
the Persians.   It was not a combat on an open battle-
field, it was not a purely defensive combat, but it was
a taking of the offensive in accordance with the edict.
Although the name of God does not occur in the Book

of Esther,[1] yet it is not wanting in religious charac-
teristics : belief in providential guidance, prayer, and
fasting.   But beyond these it reminds us of what
Jesus uttered in His criticism of the Old Testament
law and morality (Matt. v. 44) : " Ye have heard that
it was said, Thou shalt love thy neighbour, and hate
thine enemy : but I say unto you, Love your enemies,
and pray for them that persecute you." The command, " Thou shalt love thy neighbour," is found in
Lev. xix. 18 ; the second command, " Thou shalt hate
thine enemy," thus formulated, is not found anywhere,
but it is the reverse side of the passage just quoted,
since by " thy neighbour " one of the same nationality
is intended ; and the Book of Esther is a dreadful
commentary in confirmation of the hatred of enemies,
which   the   old   Judaism   claimed   as   its   right.
When   the   edict   was   published,   there   arose   in   Susa
and everywhere festive rejoicings on account of it,
which have been continued in the celebration of Purim
as a Jewish carnival until the present day.   In this
festival the self-testimony of the old religion, concerning its relative character, culminates.   It is not the
absolute religion, for neither is the true, full will of
God revealed in it, nor is the love of the neighbour
recognised as a duty of man to man as such.   In the
Book of Esther we perceive nothing of the impulses
which the exile was to give to the people in the

---

[1] Compare the reference iv. 14 : "For if thou art entirely silent at
this time, *then* deliverance and escape shall arise to the Jews from
another place " [that is, from God], etc.

direction of the New Testament, nothing of prophetic afflation.

§ 82. *The Religious War in the Time of the Seleucidæ.*

After Alexander the Great had made an end of the Persian empire (330 B.C.), the government of his successors (διάδοχοι) began, who struggled for the inheritance of the conquered countries. Seleucus I. Nicator obtained possession of Syria. His capture of Babylon on the 1st of October 312 B.C. is the beginning of the era of the Seleucidæ. Palestine was under the dominion of the Ptolemies from 301 to 198, but not without fluctuations. In the year 198, Antiochus III. the Great (223–187) slew the Egyptians at Paneas, and took from them Palestine. The possession of this country was uncertain for a time, but in the age of Antiochus IV. Epiphanes (175–164), it stood uncontested under the Syrian sovereignty. Antiochus Epiphanes was the second son of Antiochus the Great. During the reign of his eldest brother, which lasted eleven years, Seleucus IV. Philopater (187–176), he was present as a hostage in Rome, whence he returned after Heliodorus had poisoned Seleucus, and had snatched away the dominion. He sought to enlarge his kingdom at every price through the annexation of Egypt. When finally the Romans in the year 168 commanded him to cease making war upon Egypt, and he was unwillingly compelled to leave the country, he gave vent to his anger by

sending a part of his army against Jerusalem under
Apollonius. The worship of Jehovah, the observance
of the Sabbath, and circumcision, were interdicted; the
temple at Jerusalem was consecrated to Jupiter
Olympius, and the Jews were commanded to serve the
same gods as the Greeks. Then Mattathias the priest
arose, with his five sons, John, Simon, Judas, Eleazar,
and Jonathan, in the little city of Modin, north-west
of Jerusalem, in defence and support of the Israelitish
religion. The family was named from its ancestor the
Hasmonean; and Judas, who was the real hero of the
Maccabean elevation, designated himself as Judas
בן מכ"בי, which, according to the initial theory of the
origin of the name Maccabee, is equivalent to מַתִּתְיָה
כֹּהֵן בֶּן יוֹחָנָן, "Mattathias, the priest, son of Johanan." [1]
But perhaps there is united with the name an allusion
to the resemblance of his military character to a
hammer [2] (מַקָּבִי), like Charles Martel.

He began the struggle for freedom — in which
Mattathias died 166 B.C. before any success had been

---

[1] Compare *Antiquitates*, xii. 6. 1.

[2] Both of these derivations seem to me to be improbable. The name
with such an origin as is indicated by the above initial theory would
no more belong to Judas than to the rest of his brothers. The other
derivation is not favoured by Old Testament usage. Although the
figure of dashing in pieces is used several times to represent a conqueror, yet the word מַקָּב, which indicates an instrument of medium
size, is never employed in this way, but the word פַּטִּישׁ, *hammer*,
sledge (Jer. i. 23), which is also common in Aramaic and in Rabbinical
Hebrew. Compare Curtiss, *The Name Machabee*, Leipzig 1876,
pp. 16, 21–24.—C.

attained—with four victories over Apollonius, Seron, Gorgias, and Lysias, and on the 25th of Kisleu (December) 165 B.C. restored the worship of Jehovah to the temple. The Book of Daniel arose before this event, in commemoration of which the *Chanucca* festival is still celebrated (John x. 22), and before the death of Antiochus, who died after an unsuccessful campaign in interior Asia, in the Persian city of Tabæ (164 B.C.). If the Book of Daniel is really a product of the time of the Seleucidæ, the year 168 is the latest date to which its origin[1] can be assigned—the time of the invasion of Jerusalem by Apollonius, which was followed by the attempt to make the Jews adopt heathen customs.

§ 83. *The Four World-Monarchies of the Book of Daniel.*

The Book of Daniel reckons four world-empires, since it distinguishes in chapters ii. and vii. between the Median and Persian empire, which it combines in chapter viii. The fourth world-empire is the Grecian, founded by Alexander the Great. First, on the extreme horizon of the book, the Roman world-empire ascends behind the empire of Alexander's followers (διάδοχοι). The law of perspective and the interpenetration of human barriers and divine illumination

---

[1] For a full statement of Professor Delitzsch's views on the origin of this book, see his article "Daniel," in Herzog and Plitt's *Real-Encyklopadie*, vol. iii., Leipzig 1878, pp. 469-479.—C.

to which prophecy even here is subject, relieve us of
the task of ensuring the Book of Daniel the honour of
a complete map of the world's history.   According to
xi. 2, it knows only four kings of Persia,—compare the
four heads of the leopard (vii. 6),—since Xerxes and
Darius Codomannus are blended in one person; and
although we are not able to recount the ten horns (Dan.
vii. 24, compare vers. 8 and 20) exactly, yet this is
certain, that the eleventh small horn, which raises itself
against the Most High, and persecutes the holy people
unto blood, is Antiochus Epiphanes.   The book does
not know an antichrist of a final period beyond
Antiochus Epiphanes, but everywhere the utmost tribulation continues for three years and a half (vii. 25,
ix. 27, xii. 7; compare viii. 14, where the time is
reckoned from the degradation of the high priest Onias,
in August 171).   These three and a half years are
confirmed chronologically, for until the fifteenth of
Kisleu (December) of the year 145 of the Seleucidæan
era, the tribulation increased until the pollution of the
temple by Antiochus Epiphanes, who set up in it a
statue of Jupiter Olympius;[1] and on the twenty-fifth
of Kisleu of the year 148 (that is, 164 B.C.) the
purified sanctuary was reconsecrated (1 Macc. iv. 52).
Daniel beholds the final antitypical distresses together
with those of the time of the Seleucidæ.   He does not
behold both apart, and the tribulations of the time of
the Seleucidæ are concentrated in his view in the last

---

[1] The phrase βδίλυγμα ἰρημώσιως (1 Macc. i. 54) alludes to this event.
—C.

years of Antiochus, although the death of Antiochus has not yet become the end of the religious war.

§ 84. *Recognition of Redemption in the Book of Daniel.*

I. THE STATE OF THE MESSIANIC HOPE.

In the vision of the seventy weeks (Dan. ix.) the high priest is called Messiah (מָשִׁיחַ), the world-sovereign prince (נָגִיד), and the Christ of God Messiah - Prince (מָשִׁיחַ נָגִיד), as the One who combines the dignities of the anointed priest and king in Himself. On the contrary, the stone which shatters the image of the four monarchies (Dan. ii. 44) is referred to the imperishable kingdom of the final period; and, moreover, in ver. 18, in the interpretation of the One who "like a Son of man" was brought upon the clouds of heaven before "the Ancient of days" (Dan. vii. 13), who gives him the everlasting dominion over all the world, only the saints of the Most High are mentioned, not expressly the One who with reference to this prophecy called Himself the Son of man (υἱὸς ἀνθρώ-που). In chapter ix. Daniel prophesies the person of the Messiah, but in chapters ii. and vii. he combines Him with the people which is His kingdom, as in Deutero-Isaiah the conception of the Messiah is merged in the conception of the people as the servant of Jehovah,[1] and rises again from it. We recognise, too, the influence of Deutero-Isaiah in the description of

---

[1] Compare Delitzsch's *Messianic Prophecies*, Edinburgh 1880, p. 87. —C.

the future salvation (Dan. ix. 24). The hope of salvation from evil, atonement for sin, provision of an eternal righteousness, stand here in close connection with the Messianic hope.

II. THE ANTICHRIST.

Hitherto the fact has only been hinted at, that the enmity of the world against God and His Church will finally be concentrated in one person, and will end in a deadly struggle (Ps. lxviii. 22, cx. 6; Isa. xi. 4; Hab. iii. 13). The Book of Daniel prophesies this at first [1] in a most concrete way, since it indicates the antichrist as opposed to the Christ of prophecy, and describes the struggle out of which the *christocracy* of the final period is to go forth.

III. THE CHRONOMETRY.

The nearer the fulness of times approaches, the more careful prophecy is with reference to the measurement of the time. In Daniel, however, prophecy and chronology are united in a way heretofore unparalleled. The prophetic chronology of the Book of Daniel is connected with the seventy years of Jeremiah (Dan. ix. 2; compare Ezra i. 1), which are extended for him in chapter ix. to seventy weeks of years; and when after their expiration, reckoning from the fourth year of Jehoiakim (605 B.C.), the final

[1] Compare Delitzsch's *Messianic Prophecies*, pp. 68, 102-103.—C.

redemption had not yet come, it remained as a riddle referred to faith and investigation.

IV. DEMONOLOGY.

The participation of the realm of angels in human history is peculiar to the visional part of the Book of Daniel (vii.–xii.).   This new phenomenon is not unconnected with the transplantation of Israel into the heathen world; for in general the stimulating elements in the progress of the redemptive history, not only the external, but also the internal, come from the heathen world.   Polytheism is as such demoniacal, and therefore demonological, and not only theoretically directed to an interior view of the world of spirits, but also practically to breaking through the barriers between the world of men and spirits.   It could not be otherwise than that the Israel of the exile, moved by the enchantment of heathen mythology, the glimpses of heathen mantic into futurity, and the wonders of heathen magic, should become more observant than ever before of the superhuman powers which were active in heathenism.   The enrichment of the Israelitish angelology and demonology followed as a matter of course.   The real advantage of this consisted especially in a deeper view of the origin of evil.   But this new turn was not merely such in consciousness. There now began, where Israel and the heathen stood over against each other, not only as warring powers, but also as two religions contending for existence,

that conflict which is to culminate in the struggle of
the Son of Man with the prince of the world, and
which is to result not only in the salvation of Israel,
but also of the heathen.

§ 85. *The Significance of the Book of Ecclesiastes for the Redemptive History.*

If the Book of Daniel, in its present form, is a
product of the time of the Seleucidæ, then the Book
of Ecclesiastes is certainly much older.   There are
many indications which show that it arose under
Artaxerxes II. Mnemon (405–359 B.C.), who summoned
the assistance of the Athenian Conon against the
Lacedemonians.   The poor wise man who through
his wisdom saved the small city against the great
king, is perhaps Themistocles, who in the year 480
B.C. decided the defeat of the Persians in a naval
battle, and compelled them to retreat.   When we
first discuss the Book of Ecclesiastes here, it is not an
anachronism, which is detrimental to our view of the
historical development; for the apocalypse of Daniel is
a late fruit of the prophecy which has been dumb
since the time of Nehemiah, and the Book of Ecclesiastes is a late product of the canonical chokma-
literature, and takes throughout an isolated position.
There is no other Biblical book which has a like
individual and subjective character.   It is a jere-
miad upon the transitoriness and nothingness of all
earthly things, the mysteriousness of this world, the

insufficiency of human knowledge, and the divinely determined limitation of man.   But even this book is significant for the redemptive history, since the old covenant closes here with the actual confession of its inability, and furthermore since the author saves himself from his pessimistic view of the world in the expectation of a final judgment which concerns man personally, and solves the riddle of the present world.

§ 86. *Course of the Jewish History after the Death of Antiochus.*

The end of Antiochus was not yet the end of the persecuted Church.   After Antiochus' death, 164 B.C., Lysias secured the throne.   He vanquished Judas in a dreadful battle at Beth-Zacharias, but made peace when he saw that his son was threatened at home by Philip, the guardian of the son of Antiochus.   He maintained his power for a time, and then was put out of the way by Demetrius, a nephew of Antiochus, who came from Rome.   Under this Demetrius I., surnamed Soter, the religious persecution began again. His general, Bacchides, placed Alcimus in the high-priesthood, who was friendly to the Greeks ; but Judas regathered a band, who, bidding defiance to death, put Alcimus to flight.   Upon this Demetrius sent Nicanor with a great army against Judæa, and Judas smote the Syrians in two decisive battles.   The thirteenth of Adar is the Nicanor day of the Jewish calendar.   He then made a treaty with the Romans ;

but before they could come to his assistance, he was
defeated by Bacchides at Elasa (160 B.C.), and there
died a heroic death.   His youngest brother, Jonathan,
took his place, to whom Alexander Balas, the rival
king of Demetrius, granted the crown and the high-
priesthood (152 B.C.).   Jonathan was murdered (143)
by Tryphon, another rival king of Demetrius.   His
successor was his eldest brother, Simon, who joined
the party of Demetrius, and in the year 142 was freed
from tribute.   This was the first year of the era of
Simon the high priest.   He was assassinated, with two
of his sons, by his son-in-law Ptolemy, in the year
135.   The further succession of the Maccabean priestly
kings is as follows :—John Hyrcanus I. (135–106), who
subjugated the Idumeans, and compelled them to be
circumcised; Aristobulus I., the eldest son of John
Hyrcanus (105–104), who through the murder of his
mother seized the temporal dominion; Alexander
Jannai (104–78), brother of Aristobulus, a cruel
ruler, who quarrelled with the Pharisees, and was
afterwards their open enemy, but without being able
to break their dominion; Alexandra, his wife (78–69);
Aristobulus II. (69–63), who carried on war with his
brother Hyrcanus II., and who sought the help of
Pompey.   In the year 63 Jerusalem fell into the
hands of Pompey.   Aristobulus in the year 61 adorned
his entrance into Rome, marching before the triumphal
chariot of the conqueror.   Hyrcanus II. was appointed
high priest by Pompey, without the title of king.
From that time the Roman dominion dated, which

was continued in the vassal kingdom of the Herods.
In the time of Pompey the eighteen psalms arose
which received the arbitrary title, *Psalterion Salomonis,*
and which have been known since 1626 through an
Augsburg manuscript. The stranger (ἄνθρωπος ἀλλό-
τριος), the profaner of the sanctuary, who, according
to xvii. 9, removed the legitimate Jewish prince, is
Pompey, for whom a disgraceful end is prophesied
upon the mountains of Egypt (ii. 30). The seventeenth of these psalms is the most beautiful Messianic
avowal of the Maccabean age. The Messiah appears
there as a righteous, sinless, divinely instructed king, who
unites Israel and the heathen under his peaceful sceptre.

REMARK.—Pharisees and Sadducees are two parties,
of which the former leaned especially upon the people,
the latter upon the nobility of the nation, particularly
the priestly nobility. The Pharisees were called as
such פְּרוּשִׁים, *separated,* because, in distinction from the
people, they made a stricter asceticism their duty;
but they were strong not only through their legalism,
but also through their politics. Judas Galilæus
(Acts v. 37) and the later zealots were Pharisees,
although they were ultra-Pharisees. The Sadducees
have their names especially as members of the house
of Zadok, who in Ezekiel appear as the favoured
bearers of the pontificate. Their political standpoint
was the Maccabean, that is, they held to the Hasmonean ruler, even at the expense of national freedom.[1]

[1] Compare Wellhausen, *Die Pharisäer und die Sadducäer,* Greifs-
wald 1874.

§ 87. *Hindrances in the Attainment of the New Testament Goal.*

In other respects, however, the Messianic hope, after the last voices of the prophets had died away, does not manifest itself in that inward character which had become possible, but rather in that intellectual externality which, when the Messiah appeared in Jesus, made the mass of the people incapable of recognising in Him the promised One, and which rendered it uncommonly difficult, even for those who believed in Him, to accommodate themselves to the manner of His appearance and activity, without taking offence at it. The reform under Ezra and Nehemiah aimed at making the Mosaic law the ruling power of the people's life. This was attained, but not without the result, that with the letter of the law its spirit gradually passed from the consciousness of the people, and that prophecy, as the authentic interpreter of this spirit, was neglected. The Maccabean age made its contribution toward increasing the ceremonial and legal character of Judaism; for the struggle at that time concerned the external fulfilment of the law, and turned upon circumcision and regulations respecting food and worship, and involved the danger that these outward signs would be considered as of chief importance. It is characteristic that already under Jonathan (d. 143 B.C.), the youngest brother of Judas Maccabæus, the contrast between Pharisaism and Sadduceeism arose,[1] and that

---

[1] Josephus, *Antiquitates*, xiii. 5, 10.

at the time of John Hyrcanus I. (135–105 B.C.) it had already penetrated the people's life. Although Pharisaism possessed the merit of having maintained the independence of Judaism, yet it did so through a mummiform legalism. It was also unfavourable for the retention of the Messianic hope in its purity, that now for the first time the priestly family became the head of the people, and that out of gratitude they appointed the elder brother of Jonathan, Simon (143–135 B.C.), a prince and high priest for ever, until a faithful prophet should arise and should give another decision (1 Macc. xiv. 41). This first union of both offices in the year 140 was an antagonistic anticipation of the course of redemptive history, and forestalled the fulfilment of prophecy. And since under John Hyrcanus the Jewish people enjoyed a period of freedom, of prosperity, and extension of territory, such as they had not experienced since the time of David and Solomon, the recognition of their spiritual world-calling fell into the background before their political consciousness. When, after John Hyrcanus, the star of the Hasmonean dynasty gradually went down through tyranny and civil war in blood, and was outshone by the tools of the Romans, Antipater (d. 43 B.C.) and his son Herod (37–4 B.C.), the people hoped to find in the Messiah only a king who would free them from the Roman yoke, in the same way as the Maccabees had freed them from the Seleucidæ.

REMARK.—Together with the expression of the Messianic hope in the seventeenth psalm of Solomon's

Psalter may be classed the Messianic passages of the
Sibylline book iii. 652–794; also a younger passage
of the Sibyllines, iii. 36–92, announces the future of
a sacred ruler, who will quickly bring the entire earth
under his sceptre. But no Messianic word can be
discovered in the Apocrypha of the Alexandrian codex.
It is only said that an eternal kingdom is promised to
the house of David (Sirach xlvii. 11, 1 Macc. ii. 57.) The
Assumptio Mosis prophesies indeed a kingdom of God,
but without the Messiah; and the book of *Jubilees*
indulges in descriptions of the glory of the final period,
but the ruler is the congregation of the servants of
God, and nothing is said respecting the Messiah.
This need not surprise us, for the prevailing representation of the Messiah was not according to every one's
taste.   The Messiah was conceived of solely as a king
sent by God, who through a bloody struggle breaks the
way to everlasting peace, not, as might have been
expected from the final prophetic voices, as the bodily
presence of God, not as the One who offers Himself
that He may become the Mediator of redemption.
The age of the Maccabees threw the Messianic hope
back again into the stadium of the one-sided royal
image, which appears as surpassed in Deutero-Isaiah,
Zechariah, and Malachi.   In Philo, too, it is not otherwise, but his doctrine of the Logos contains thoughts
which were fitted to breathe a new life into the image
of the Messiah, a life corresponding to the spirit of
prophecy.

§ 88. *New Testament Germs in the Post-Canonical Books of Wisdom.*

The Book of Ecclesiastes stands midway between the canonical literature of the chokma, which it completes, and that which is apocryphal and post-Biblical. The fundamental idea of this literature is wisdom itself. Already in the addresses of the Book of Proverbs (i.–ix.) an hypostatic existence is attributed to it, which approaches personality. Even the comparison that wisdom is equivalent to God's Son appears to be drawn already in Prov. xxx. 4,[1] as well as in the expressions concerning God's word (Ps. cvii. 20, cv. 19; Isa. lv. 10 sq.), and thus prepares the way for hypostasizing the word. The development of the idea of wisdom is continued in the Palestinian Apocrypha, for example in Sirach xxiv., compare li. 10, but especially in the Alexandrian Book of the Wisdom of Solomon. When here in chaps. vii.–ix. "an only-begotten Spirit" ($\pi\nu\epsilon\hat{u}\mu\alpha$ $\mu o\nu o\gamma\epsilon\nu\acute{\eta}s$) is assigned to wisdom (*sophia*), when she is called the "effulgence of the eternal light" ($\dot{a}\pi\alpha\acute{u}\gamma\alpha\sigma\mu\alpha$ $\phi\omega\tau\grave{o}s$ $\alpha\dot{\iota}\omega\nu\acute{\iota}ov$), and "the image of his goodness" ($\epsilon\dot{\iota}\kappa\grave{\omega}\nu$ $\tau\hat{\eta}s$ $\dot{a}\gamma\alpha\theta\acute{o}\tau\eta\tau os$ $\alpha\dot{u}\tau o\hat{u}$), it is easy to see whither this development is tending, for wisdom (*sophia*) appears as a participant in the creation of the world (Sirach ix. 9); she is called a sharer of God's throne,

---

[1] "Who hath ascended up into heaven, or descended? who hath gathered the wind in His fists? who hath bound the waters in a garment? who hath established all the ends of the earth? what is His name, and what is His Son's name, if thou canst tell?"

(Sirach ix. 4, πάρεδρος); and the author of the book prays that God will send her to him, that she may be with him, work with him, and make known God's will to him (Sirach ix. 10 sq.). Word (λόγος) and wisdom (σοφία) are even here synonyms (Sirach ix. 1 sq.; compare xxiv. 3). According to x. 17, it was wisdom which led Israel in the pillar of cloud and of fire. In the Targums the constant expression for God in His revelation of Himself to the world is the "word of Jehovah" (מֵימְרָא דַיְהֹוָה), and even in the Palestinian theology "word" and "wisdom" are cognate ideas; but it was Egypt rather than Palestine where the way for the Christological conception was prepared.

REMARK.—The Targum uses the expression Word of God instead of God, (1) when mention is made of God's feelings in an anthropopathic way, for example, Gen. vi. 6, "It repented Jehovah," which Onkelos renders, "Jehovah changed His mind in His Logos;" (2) when revelations of God in the world are related, for example, Gen. iii. 8, "They heard the voice of Jehovah Elohim," for which Onkelos has, "They heard the voice of the Logos of Jehovah." For מֵימְרָא the word דִּבּוּרָא is found in the Jerusalem Targum; for example, Num. vii. 89, according to which it was the Word (דִּבּוּרָא) which spoke with Moses from the covering of the ark of the covenant. A related and almost similar conception is the synagogal Shekinah (שְׁכִינָה), that is, the dwelling of God with His people in this world, His gracious presence, and especially His presence in the temple between the cherubim

(Ps. xxvi. 8 ; 3 Macc. ii. 15 sq. ; compare 1 Sam. iv. 21).
The Targum uses this word, Gen. iii. 24 ; Ex. xvi. 7,
where the glory of Jehovah (כְּבוֹד יְהוָה) is translated
"the glory of His Shekinah."   When the Gospel of
John, i. 14, says, "The Word became flesh and taber-
nacled among us," it indicates Jesus Christ as the
bodily Shekinah of God ; and when in the *Sayings of
the Jewish Fathers*, iii. 3, it is said, "Two that sit
together and discuss the words of the Tora have the
Shekinah among them,"[1] this sounds remarkably
like Matt. xviii. 20. The New Testament idea of
the Logos is not new ; but this is new, that Jesus
is indicated as the Word who has become flesh, and as
the wisdom of God which has appeared in human form.
Everything which prophecy and the chokma-literature
saw concerning God as historically revealed, in distinction from God as the transcendent primitive source, finds
in Jesus Christ, according to Col. ii. 9, its final unity.

§ 89. *The Jewish Alexandrinism.*

The greater part of those who emigrated with Jeremiah may have fallen a prey to the judgments with
which the prophet (Jer. xliv. 11–14) threatened them ;
but afterwards Alexander the Great attracted Jewish
settlers to the city of Alexandria, which was founded
by him. And Ptolemæus Lagi (311–285 B.C.), subsequently to the conquest of Jerusalem, again brought a
multitude of Jews to Egypt. After Antiochus had

[1] Compare Taylor, *Sayings of the Jewish Fathers*, Cambridge 1877.

taken possession of Palestine (314 B.C.), many Jews went thither of their own accord. Although the possession of Egypt was for a long time in dispute between the Ptolemies and the Seleucidæ, yet Palestine was mostly Egyptian; for it was again and again reconquered by the Ptolemies. The numerous colonies of Jews to Egypt are partially due to this fact. They lived there in happy circumstances. The prophecy of Isaiah xix. 18 sq. seemed to be realized. Here in Egypt under Ptolemy Philadelphus (284–247 B.C.), perhaps already toward the end of the reign of his father, Ptolemy Lagi, the translation of the Holy Scriptures into Greek began with the Tora. Thus arose the language of future Christianity, and the Old Testament Scriptures now preached, although with stammering tongue, to the heathen also. Here, through the collision of Judaism and Hellenism, the Palestinian chokma developed into a religious philosophy, which was brought to the highest stage of development by Philo, who lived contemporaneously with the beginning of Christianity, without becoming acquainted with it. This philosophy of religion lost in many things the Biblical truth through Hellenistic influences, and unfortunately introduced, for the reconciliation of Hellenistic and Israelitic modes of thought, the allegorical method of interpretation, which for a long time brought error into the understanding of the Scriptures; nevertheless it was recognised by Christianity itself as a link in the chain of its providential preparation. The Logos of Philo is hypostatic; he is God's Son,

he is a being who enters into a real ethical relation
to man, rescuing the soul sunk in sensuality through the
power of the divine mercy, and giving himself as high
priest, paraclete, teacher, and leader, physician, and
shepherd. He is the angel of the Lord, standing
above the angels; he is God, as he attested himself
through the medium of angels in the life of the patriarchs, and in the history of Israel.

REMARK 1.—The thought of an incarnation of the
Logos is absolutely inconceivable for Philo, and he
positively denies, in several passages, that the Godhead
and the sublime Logos can descend into bodily neces-
sities.[1] Moreover, all the premisses are wanting in
Philo which are necessary even for an anticipation of
the mystery, " The Word became flesh," for—

(1) He has no insight into the fact of the fall, and
into the necessity of the divine act of an objective
salvation. He has nothing to say about a historical
development of salvation by the reciprocal relation of
God and man; he considers the relation of God to the
world which is mediated through the Logos as always
objectively the same.

(2) The Messiah remains in his system completely
in the background. It is true that he firmly maintains the Messianic hope, and describes the time of the
Messiah with sensuous colours; but that hope does not
enter into connection with the doctrine of the Logos.

[1] See Delitzsch, *Messianic Prophecies*, Edinburgh 1880, p. 115,
Rem., and his article " Johannes und Philo," in the *Zeitschrift für die
gesammte Lutherische Theologie*, Leipzig 1863, pp. 219–229.

(3) A merging of the Logos in the flesh must necessarily horrify him, because from his point of view man as man is sinful, and the body as such is a source of evil.

REMARK 2.—The trinitarian conception of God is not a product of philosophical speculation, but the reflex, not only of New Testament, but also even of the Old Testament facts of revelation. God and the Spirit of God are already distinguished upon the first page of the Holy Scriptures, and between both the Angel of God stands as the Mediator of the covenant after Gen. xvi., and as the leader of Israel after Ex. xiv. 19; the Angel of His presence, according to Isa. lxiii. 9, is the Saviour (מוֹשִׁיעַ) of His people.[1] But as God in the course of the Old Testament history represents Himself as God the Redeemer in His Angel, so prophecy predicts a future man in whom God the Redeemer represents Himself in bodily form. If now we add to God, who is the primitive source of all things, and to God's Spirit the immanence of God in His Angel, and in the New Testament sense in His Christ, we thus have a trinity in God's unity. Deuteronomy uses, instead of the expression the "Angel of His presence," simply "His presence" (Deut. iv. 37), as also the other Semitic religions distinguish God's face from the hidden God, that is, the manifestation of Himself with respect to the world. The doctrine of

[1] Jacob in his benediction upon Ephraim and Manasseh, Gen. xlix. 15, 16, says, "God, before whom my fathers Abraham and Isaac did walk, the God which fed me all my life long unto this day, the Angel which redeemed me from all evil, bless the lads," etc.

the Logos is nothing else than the evolution of that which is involved in " His face." And the dogma of the trinity is an attempt to combine those facts and utterances of revelation by means of reflection, and to ensure them against becoming shallow and distorted.

§ 90. *The Threshold of the Fulfilment.*

Nothing is now wanting but that the Logos of God should step forth from the realm of human representation into historical reality, and in a way which was incomprehensible for Philo, that is, in a human body. Nothing is wanting but that wisdom which appears as a preacher in Proverbs i.-ix., which attests herself as a child of God, as a mediatress in the creation of the world, as a lover of man, should take on flesh and blood, by uniting herself personally with a son of David, and that this wisdom which has become man should work out the redemption which causes the shrill lamentations to cease, with which the old covenant in the Book of Ecclesiastes sings its own burial song. This begins to be fulfilled on the boundary of the second half of this sixth period. As in the second half of the sixth day of creation man was formed, so the Son of man proceeds from mankind, through whom the human history recommences. So long, however, as this divine Son of the woman, whom the Protevangelium has in view, is not yet born through death into the new life of glory, the old covenant is still dominant, and the Old Testament history of redemption still continues.

SIXTH PERIOD.

§ 91. *The Incarnation.*

THE " fulness of times " ($\pi\lambda\acute{\eta}\rho\omega\mu\alpha$ $\tau\hat{\omega}\nu$ $\kappa\alpha\iota\rho\hat{\omega}\nu$) has
now come. As the world of the creation, so
the world of the completion stands in God's eternal
consciousness as a finished whole. But as the world
of the creation, so also the world of the completion
could not otherwise be actualized than by a gradual
succession of periods. These times ($\kappa\alpha\iota\rho o\acute{\iota}$), whose
extent, sequence, and contents omniscience determines,
with an educational purpose, have now become full.
The history of fulfilment itself draws from the given
premisses the conclusion, through which all riddles in
the formation of the Old Testament history are solved,
and both of the convergent lines of the Old Testament
proclamation of redemption are brought together. In
Jesus the Christ, Jehovah and the Son of David become
one. Heaven and earth interpenetrate, that they may
unite in Him and be united by Him. For He is, as
Isa. iv. prophesies, not only the " Sprout (צֶמַח) of

180

Jehovah," who, like a noble twig from heaven, is planted in the earth, but also the "fruit (פְּרִי) of the ground," in whom all the growth and bloom of earthly history attains its divinely intended and predicted maturity.

REMARK 1. — It is especially Matthew's Gospel which aims to show that Jesus, who appeared in the fulness of times, is the fulfiller of law and prophecy. The genealogy, Matt. i., divides the *prehistory* of Jesus Christ into forty-two generations, which form three groups. The first group begins with Abraham, for his election is the beginning of the people of promise, from whom Jesus was to be born. The second group begins with David, for David's elevation as king is the beginning of the kingdom of promise, which in Christ is to become an eternal kingdom of boundless extent. The third group begins with the age after the carrying away into captivity, for with this event the sorrowful time begins in which the kingdom of the promise, blooming again in Zerubbabel, withers, in order that in the fulness of times the ripe fruit may appear instead of the flower of preparation and promise. In reply to the question why Matthew reckons forty-two generations,—that is, three times fourteen,—perhaps Surenhusius (d. 1720) has given the right answer. The name David (דָּוִד) amounts, according to the value of its letters, to fourteen. The evangelist, therefore, appears in a secret way to have stamped the name David upon the prehistory in all its three groups.

REMARK 2.—Matthew begins, like another Tora,

with the words, " The book of the generation of Jesus
Christ." The wonderful name Christ is first added to
the proper name Jesus after He had shown Himself
to be the divinely consecrated king whom the Old
Testament predicted (Acts ii. 26). But the evan-
gelists write the double name Jesus Christ above the
portals of their Gospels (Mark i. 1 ; John i. 17) as
an anagram or emblem of the entire following history,
similarly as the Tora stamps the name Jehovah Elohim
as such an anagram upon the entrance of the sacred
history. The name Jesus was in the post-exilic
time a common Jewish name : יֵשׁוּעַ is equivalent to
יְהוֹשֻׁעַ, for which reason the Septuagint transcribes
the name of Joshua as ʼΙησοῦς.

It is characteristic—

(1) That the Lord did not have an exceptional
name, for He was a man, and as such a member of a
people, a child of an age and of a country.

(2) That this name, however, is the most fitting
that He could have had. It signifies Jehovah is salvation, and as the name of the Lord : the bearer and
the mediator of salvation. The designation is prepared by such passages as Gen. xlix. 18, Isa. xlix. 6,
lii. 10, especially in the Book of Isaiah ; even the
name of this prophet signifies the salvation of Jehovah,
or Jehovah saves. The name Christ united with
Jesus, is made a proper name by the omission of the
article, as Elohim in the designation Jehovah Elohim
becomes a proper name in the same way.

REMARK 3.—The incarnation is a mystery, whose

essence we can better determine negatively than positively. With the person of Christ, as the prophets already predicted, God is united in a unique way. It is not only a mystical union (*unio mystica*), like His union with the prophets and other men of God; not a sacramental union (*unio sacramentalis*), as His presence was connected with the ark of the covenant; but a personal union (*unio personalis*), since the mediating Logos, who mirrors the being of God, made a human consciousness in Christ the form of His own.

REMARK 4.—The miracle of the beginning of the life of Jesus, His birth through the Holy Ghost, and the close of His life, His resurrection, stand in a polar reciprocity; and these two miracles, even aside from their historical attestation, are postulates of faith. For if Jesus is the ideal man who is to redeem mankind, who have fallen from their ideal, and is to attain for them the power of a completion corresponding to this ideal, He could neither be born as flesh from flesh, nor dying see corruption.

§ 92. *The Herald and his Ordination.*

The spirit of prophecy departed from Israel after Malachi. It was in vain in the Maccabean struggles that the people looked anxiously for a faithful prophet whom God should raise up (1 Macc. xiv. 41). Now, however, on the boundary of the old and new covenant, after prophecy had been silent four hundred years, Israel again received in John the Baptist a prophet

who was counted worthy of the greatest honour since
Samuel, and who was the voice in the wilderness
which had been predicted in Isa. xl. 3, a second
Elijah, according to the prophecy of Malachi. The
baptism of John ensured the expectation of the
entrance into the kingdom of heaven. Even Jesus
submitted to it. It was His anointing (Acts x. 38)
for His calling through the Holy Spirit without
measure (Col. i. 19, compare John iii. 34); and as the
designated king of the heavenly kingdom received
this baptism, it took on the form of an event which
far transcended its usual character. The Spirit, which
hovered over the waters of the *tohu* (Gen. i. 2), flew
down upon the moistened head of the Son of man,
who was to become the mediator of a new creation,
and God recognised Him as His beloved Son.

REMARK 1.—While the testimony of Josephus concerning Jesus the Christ[1] can only have been written
by a Christian, the genuineness of his testimony concerning John the Baptist[2] is undoubted. He speaks
of John the Baptist with great respect. He calls him
a good man, who exhorted the Jews to virtue and
piety, and made previous purification of the soul
through righteousness a condition of his baptism.
The people gathered about him, and had great satisfaction in listening to his words. They honoured him
so much, that they regarded the victory of Aretas

---

[1] *Antiquitates*, xviii. 3, 3, compare xx. 9, 1. Eusebius, *Historia
ecclesiastica*, i. 11.

[2] *Antiquitates*, xviii. 5, 2.

over Herod the tetrarch as the punishment which came upon him on account of his execution of the Baptist.

REMARK 2.—The preaching of the Baptist, which was continued by Jesus, had as its theme, " Repent ye ; for the kingdom of heaven is at hand." The designation "kingdom of heaven," which corresponds to the old synagogal מַלְכוּת שָׁמַיִם, is exclusively peculiar to the first Gospel. The other Gospels use the expression "kingdom of God" for it, according to which kingdom of heaven is equivalent to a kingdom which has its origin in heaven, and is of a heavenly character. In the Old Testament, the theocratic relation of God to Israel was a type and primary step to this kingdom, which the prophets beheld before partly as a kingdom of the immediate dominion of Jehovah, partly as a kingdom of the dominion of His Anointed. The announcement that the kingdom from above is near aroused the expectation that the victorious, beneficent, glorious dominion of God and His Christ would soon begin. Even John the Baptist himself thought so, for he was as a prophet subject to the law of perspective, and he saw the kingdom which he proclaimed at the summit of its completion, without knowing the intermediate stations and the deep way through the valley to the goal. It is not strange that he refused to baptize Jesus, for it was a riddle to him how the Anointed of the kingdom of heaven could accept this consecration from one who awaited that kingdom.

REMARK 3.—The reasons why Jesus submits to the baptism of John are the following:—

(1) The Sinless One submits to the baptism of repentance,—

(a) Because He is not only apparently, but also really, born a member of the people for whom the baptism of John is ordained as a means of sanctifying initiation into the kingdom of heaven.

(b) He can submit to it, because although He is without sin, yet He is not without a human nature, which is affected by the consequences of sin ; in brief, because He has entered into a solidarity with sinful man.

(2) The King of the heavenly kingdom submits to the baptism which constitutes a claim to that kingdom, in so far as the initiation for the coming kingdom of heaven can be at the same time an initiation for its coming King, who, like the kingdom of heaven itself, ascends from humility to glory.

§ 93. *The Victor over the Tempter.*

The Messiah's consecration is followed by a test, and this test takes on such a form that the relation of the history of Jesus becomes evident not only to the history of Israel, but also to that of mankind. Israel, the people of salvation, God's first-born, was tried forty years in the wilderness, but yielded time after time to its lusts, and proved itself, with a few exceptions, to be incompetent for its calling. The first human pair

were tried in Paradise, where the divine love surrounded them with a thousand evidences of its reality.
Yet they fell from the relation in which the Creator
had placed them to Himself, instead of ratifying it by
an actual recognition. But Jesus, the Man of Salvation,
God's only-begotten Son, the second Adam, overcomes
all the attacks of the evil one, which after forty days
of spiritual conflict reached their climax, and proves
Himself to be the One who is to accomplish Israel's
redemptive calling, and to restore in a transcendent
way that which was lost through Adam.

REMARK.—Forty is the number indicating continuance under similar conditions between polar extremes,
—the number of the time of waiting, of the crisis, of the
way to the goal. The following are examples :—Forty
days Goliath stands over against the camp of Israel
challenging them, until the son of Jesse comes
(1 Sam. xvii. 16). Forty days Moses lingers upon
Mount Sinai, neither eating nor drinking, until he
receives the tables of the covenant (Ex. xxiv. 18,
xxxiv. 28). According to the same principle, forty
days also pass between the resurrection and ascension.
This rhythmical return of forty days really seems to
be, as John Peter Lange (b. 1802) has remarked, a
secret law of historical life.

§ 94. *The Legislator.*

Jesus appeared as a prophet like Moses, preaching
on the mountain the programme of the kingdom, and

giving a better Tora instead of the Sinaitic. As the Book of the Covenant (Ex. xx.-xxiii.) is the fundamental compendium of the Sinaitic Tora, so the Sermon on the Mount is the fundamental compendium of the Zionitic Tora (Isa. xlii. 4, compare ii. 3). The good and holy essence of the Old Testament law, on account of the unbroken natural character of Israel, had to be fixed in stone letters; and since it could only appear at first as a sanctifying order of life of a single people, it enters into national barriers. The preacher on the mount shatters both these phenomenal forms,—the literal and the national,—and releases its good and holy substance, that is, the spirit of the law. With the words, "But I say unto you," He sets His legislative will against not only the Pharisaic ordinances, but also against the Old Testament appointments of the law; for God, who gave a law on Sinai to Israel, is in Him, and does not now give a law from the cloud in the midst of thunder and lightning, but through man's mouth for man.

REMARK.—The Sermon on the Mount begins with ten benedictions, which correspond to the ten fundamental words of the Old Testament Tora, for the word μακάριοι, "blessed," is repeated nine times (Matt. v. 3-11), and the tenth time (ver. 12) it is transformed into the sonorous finale, χαίρετε καὶ ἀγαλλιᾶσθε, "Rejoice and be exceeding glad." The four first makárioi relate to the condition and disposition of the citizens of the kingdom: poverty, sorrow, meekness, aspiration; the three following relate to their chief virtues: mercy, purity of heart, peaceableness; and

the three last to their lot in this world : ignominy,
persecution, calumny.   The Sermon on the Mount
contains in an elementary manner all the essential
parts of the New Testament doctrine of the person of the
Redeemer, His work, and the way of salvation.   The
relation in which they stand forth and recede is con-
ditioned through the law of progress, under which not
only Jesus' work, but also His person was placed.

§ 95. *The Worker of Miracles.*

But Jesus prepares the coming kingdom of heaven
not only by preaching, but also by working ; and as
His word, so also His miracles are anticipatory repre-
sentations of the new order of things.   Sin brought
death, and has therewith subjugated man to disease,
which is ever a tendency to death.   It has made him
as one in bondage, subject to the dominion of evil.
It has estranged him from the natural world, and this
from him.   What is now the object of the appearance
and the goal of Christ's work ?   To overcome sin,
death, and the devil, and to liberate man from spiritual
and bodily evil ; to make the one in bondage free, and
the servant a master.   Everywhere the miracle appears
as the necessary supplement of the proclamation ; the
word indicates the way of salvation, the miracle manifests the bringer of salvation, and actually shows what
faith has to expect from Him.

REMARK.—It is an error when Hegel indicates this
as the chief standpoint of reason, that the spiritual

cannot become externally accredited but only through
and in itself. The same view is also found in
Chrysostom.[1] But the miracle not only serves for the
confirmation of a truth which is external to it; it is
not only a means, it is itself an end. Miracles prove
that Jesus is what He is. They are preludes of His
work in its completion.

§ 96. *The Mediator.*

It is a necessity for one who loves a man with his
entire soul to direct all the power of his activity for
his good; and when he can promote this good through
the acceptance of hardship, of suffering, nay, when
through his death he can preserve the life of such a
friend, love makes this suffering a rapture for him. Thus
Jesus loved not this or that man more than another—
He loved man. He saw man under the bondage of
evil, fettered by sin, under the ban of death; and since
He knew that He was free from sin, He determined
to put Himself at the head of sinful humanity as its
representative before God, to take all the guilt and its
consequences upon His heart and conscience; and that
thereby man might become free from wrath and hell,
He determined to plunge into the abyss of both, that

---

[1] *Opera*, Benedictine edition, vol. v. p. 271 : τοὺς παχυτέρους διεγείρων
διὰ τῶν τερασσίων, ὁ μὲν γὰρ ὑψηλὸς καὶ φιλόσοφος οὐδὲν δεήσεται τῶν σημείων.
μακάριοι γὰρ οἱ μὴ ἰδόντες καὶ πιστεύσαντες. " He was awakening the
most fleshly by means of the miraculous, for the noble and the philo-
sopher do not need signs ; for blessed are they that have not seen, and
yet have believed."

it might be shut. The history of the world knows no friend of man like Him. Even if Jews and heathen had not murdered Him by joining hands, His compassionate, ardent love for man would have consumed Him like a burning fever. The thought of offering Himself to God, that man might again become an object of God's favour, ruled His entire inward and outward life; and His unique origin from God was not detrimental to the reality of the passion, but rather intensified its anguish; for the more tender the body is, the greater is its susceptibility to pain, and the more the soul thirsts for love, the more deeply it feels its rejection by God and men. The fact that in Gethsemane grief and trembling seized upon Him, and momentarily dimmed His consciousness concerning the necessity of His dying, can only be explained by supposing that He looked down into the very depths of His impending death as the decree of God's wrath. He was not afraid of death in itself, but of the death in which the sins of man and the furious assault of Satan would do their utmost to destroy Him, and in which He would feel the entire weight of God's wrath, which He sought to propitiate; in a word, He was afraid of the bruise which He was to receive from the serpent in His heel. As He cried out on the cross, "My God, My God, why hast Thou forsaken Me?" He came, in being thus forsaken by God, to taste the curse which would have fallen upon us, if in the midst of this utmost strain upon the trinitarian relation He had not held fast the divine love and won us back.

§ 97. *The Destruction of the Old Covenant.*

According to the Gospel of John (xix. 14), it was the day of preparation for the passover (עֶרֶב פֶּסַח), upon which Jesus was delivered to the death of a traitor and of a slave on the cross. If, according to the fourth Gospel, the eve of the passover was at the same time the eve of the Sabbath in the passion week, then, according to the Mishna,[1] the slaughtering of the evening lamb of the continual burnt-offering (*tamid*) had already begun at half-past six o'clock, or, as we reckon, at half-past twelve in the afternoon. The evening lamb was then offered at half-past seven (1.30 P.M.), and immediately afterward followed the slaughtering of the passover lambs. Hence at the time when in the temple the blood of the evening lamb and of the passover lambs was flowing, there bled upon the cross the true Tamid, that is, the offering which has everlasting efficacy (Heb. x. 14), and the true Passover, or the sacrifice which makes us inaccessible to the destroyer, and causes us to be spared. In the temple the service of the shadow was still in vogue, but outside, where, in spite of the time of the full moon, the heavens were darkened at midday, the blood, which covered the pure body of the Holy One of God, announced, like the roseate hues of the morning, a new day. This depth of His suffering is the turning-point of both Testaments. The old covenant first dies to

[1] *Pesachim*, sec. v. 1.

rise again as the new, when Jesus dies through the law to the law in order to rise again to an unbounded life.

REMARK.—The beginning and end of the Sabbath and of the feast days were determined by the astronomical time of day; besides, night and day were each reckoned at twelve hours. The nocturnal half of the day of twenty-four hours began in the evening at six o'clock, and the daily half at six in the morning, so that the hour from twelve to one corresponds to our morning hour from six to seven, and the hour from six to seven to our hour from twelve to one in the afternoon; hence seven and a half o'clock, according to the Palestinian reckoning, is equivalent to half-past one o'clock according to our reckoning.

SEVENTH PERIOD.

FROM JESUS' ENTOMBMENT UNTIL HIS RESURRECTION. THE CONCLUDING SABBATH OF THE OLD TESTAMENT HISTORY.

§ 98. *The Sabbath of the Creator and the Sabbath of the Redeemer.*

THIS seventh period is a space of one day and a portion of two others. But as Moses (Ps. xc. 4) says, a thousand years in the sight of God are as a day, so Peter (2 Pet. iii. 8) with equal propriety says, "One day is with the Lord as a thousand years" —these three scant days outweigh centuries. They form the transition from the Old Testament history to the New, as the Sabbath of creation is the transition from the creation of the world to the subsequent history of that world. All the Gospels agree that it was a Friday (*paraskeue*) on which the Saviour was crucified. On a Friday the Redeemer ended His sufferings, and here as there followed upon this Friday a Sabbath, which there was the dividing wall between the creation of the world and the world's history; here it is the dividing wall between conflict and victory, suffering and reward of suffering, attainment of salva-

194

tion and its consummation. Until then there stood side by side the old covenant which was still in force, and the new covenant which was in process of formation.

§ 99. *The Sign of the Prophet Jonah.*

As God proved through Jonah that His intention in the call of a prophet could not be nullified by anything, so He will prove it through Jesus. The One who was supposed to be dead will appear to the terror of this generation, which demands a sign. But the significance of the sign, Matt. xii. 39 sq., extends farther. As Jonah, so Jesus who has passed through a three days' grave turns to the heathen: Jonah, since in the midst of the Old Covenant he accomplishes a more New Testament than an Old Testament mission; Jesus, since as the Risen One He begins the new covenant, of which He Himself is the bond, by sending His disciples to every creature under heaven. The entire significance of the sign is concentrated in the fact, that the salvation of the world, which breaks through the previous national barriers, goes forth from the death which Jesus suffers at the hands of the Jews.

REMARK.—The Book of Jonah is like a dove sent out from Israel, which brings the heathen the olive branch of peace. It is a self-justification of the God of Israel, against the mistake that He is the exclusive, national God of the Jews. That which is typical in

the conduct and suffering of Jonah consists in the fact
that it is Jewish narrowness which renders him dis-
obedient to God's command.   It is likewise Jewish
narrowness which commits the judicial murder on the
Saviour of the world.   Judaism condemned itself in
putting the Holy One of God to death.   Dead through
Judaism to Judaism, that is, removed beyond the
national barriers, the Risen One turns to the heathen,
until the recognition scene between Joseph and his
brethren shall be typically repeated between Jesus and
the people of Israel.[1]

§ 100. *The Mysterious Word concerning the Rebuilding
of the Temple.*

" Destroy the temple," said Jesus, " and in three
days I will raise it up " (John ii. 19).   " He spake,"
as the evangelist adds, " of the temple of His body."
But in what connection does the temple of His body
stand with the temple whose cleansing he had just
accomplished ?   His body was the destruction of this

---

[1] The following beautiful comparison is given in Baumgarten's
Theologischer Commentar zum Pentateuch, Kiel 1843, pp. 345, 346 :
" As Joseph betrayed [by his brethren] first became a ruler in Egypt,
and as such saved the Egyptians from destruction, while his father
supposed he was dead and his brethren went about under the curse of
their guilt, so too Christ crucified first becomes a king of the heathen,
while His brethren wander disheartened under the curse of His blood,
which cries to heaven.   But when the fulness of the heathen shall have
been brought into the kingdom of salvation, then in the deepest privacy,
without the presence of a stranger, He will make Himself known to
His brethren, and then all Egypt shall know that the Lord of Egypt is
the son and brother of Israel."

stone temple, and His resurrection was the raising up of a new spiritual temple, whose fundamental and efficacious beginning is the Risen One Himself, for "the Church is His body, the fulness of Him that filleth all in all" (Eph. i. 23). The enigmatical word of Jesus hints at the fulfilment of Zech. vi. 12 sq., and at the same time of Hos. vi. 2. As He went forth from the grave the temple arose, whose foundation and corner-stone is Himself. His "quickening" was at the same time the quickening (compare Eph. ii. 5; Col. ii. 13) of His Church, which is a regenerated congregation from Israel and all nations. F. C. Baur[1] (b. 1792, d. 1860) says: the temple made with hands (Mark xiv. 58) is the real temple; the three days refer to the resurrection, and the expression "not made with hands" refers to the resurrection and the new spiritual religion. But we say that it refers to the Risen One and the Church, which, according to 1 Cor. vi. 19, 2 Cor. vi. 16, is His body, and the temple of the Holy Spirit.

§ 101. *The Attainment of the Prophetical Progress to Rest.*

The Sabbath when Jesus was in His grave is the transition from an old Israel to a new, from the congregation of the law to the congregation of the new birth; it is the conclusion of the Old Testament his-

[1] *Kritische Untersuchungen über die Kanonischen Evangelien*, Tübingen 1847, p. 141.

tory.   This history presented itself to us as a typical
progress, independent of conscious human volition, and
accompanied by the revelation in words, whose contents and measure is determined in a pedagogical way
according to the comprehension and need of the
recipient.   This twofold process has now found its
conclusion; prophecy has reached its goal in Him who
is the fulfilment of the prophecy of Malachi concerning
the angel of the covenant back to the protevangelium.
The parallel converging series of prophecies, announcing the parousia of Jehovah and the parousia of the
second David, have been united in the person of the
God-man Christ.   The Servant of Jehovah has now
offered Himself, and the depth of His humiliation has
become the beginning of His exaltation.   The root of
Jesse will now soon stand as a banner for the nations.
The Son of Abraham has become a curse in order to
become a blessing to all the families of the earth.
The Son of the woman has endured the bruise in the
heel from the serpent; but He sank to conquer, and
rose from the dead that He might share God's throne,
until all His enemies should be made His footstool.

§ 102. *The Attainment of the Typical Progress to*
Rest.

The murder by Cain is accomplished, and the blood
of the second Abel cries.   The second Noah has
entered into the ark of the grave, and will soon send
forth a dove, which shall announce that a new world

has arisen from the waters. Isaac has left the sacrificial wood, Golgotha has become another Moriah. Jacob-Israel has ceased to wrestle, and has won the blessing. Judah has come to Shiloh, the place of rest. David has patiently endured, and will soon reign as Solomon, and minister like Melchizedek. Elisha, " the chariot of Israel and the horsemen thereof," is buried, but in his bones the powers of life are active. Thus all the types as well as prophecies of the Old Testament now celebrate in Him their Sabbath. The Servant of Jehovah, torn by anguish and judgment, has entered into peace, and rests in his narrow chamber. The Good Shepherd has made the grave His bed, after His unthankful people had pierced Him; but it is really the sword of Jehovah which has smitten Him. The sword of Jehovah has smitten Him, but love has guided the sword of wrath; for this death is designed to be our life, these wounds are to be the fountains of our salvation. The seed-corn of Paradise now lies in the stillness of the earth. He rests in God's love, and His repose in death is life. The race of the flood, the spirits in prison, see the Living One, and in His hand the keys of hell and death. But the congregation below, which is to be, waits for the sign of Jonah. It prays with Habakkuk (iii. 2), " Revive Thy work in the midst of the years;" and hopes with Hosea (vi. 2), " On the third day He will raise us up, and we shall live before Him." The resurrection is the *fiat lux* (let there be light) of a new spiritual creation. The Sunday of the resurrection is the daybreak of the New

Testament history. For since now the new man, the second Adam, has come, the re-establishment of a new humanity begins. The redemption is completed, and the gathering and perfection of the redeemed now begins.

INDICES.

INDEX I.

NAMES AND SUBJECTS.

ABEL, 30, 32.

Abram—Abraham, separation from heathen world, 41 ; relation to Melchizedek, 42 ; object of his call, 43 ; the father of believers, 44 ; relation to the nations, 48 ; a prophet, 48 ; his life a progress from faith to faith, 50 ; significance of name, 51 ; covenant with, 52.

Achæmenidæ, 149, 151.

Adam, potencies of sin and grace, 30 ; history of, 32 ; daughters, 32 ; signification of name, 34.

Adar, 151, 157, 167.

Agur, 123.

Ahaz, 120, 123, 124.

Ahaziah, 111.

Ahijah, 105.

Ahithophel, 89, 90.

Ahriman, serpent creature of, 26.

Aibu, 26.

Alexander Balas, 168.

Alexander the Great, 159, 161.

Amos, 117.

Amosis, 55.

Amram, signification of name, 56.

Angel of Jehovah, 45, 46.

Angelology, 165.

Angelophanies, 45, 155.

Animal sacrifices, depreciation of, 117.

Antichrist, 145, 162, 164.

Antiochus III. the Great, 159.

Antiochus IV. Epiphanes, 159, 162, 167.

Antipater, 171.

Apollonius, 160, 161.

Aretas, 184.

Artaxerxes I. Longimanus, 151, 152, 156.

Artaxerxes II. Mnemon, 166.

Assumptio Mosis, 172.

Assyria, 121, 122, 124, 125 sq.

Asuriddili, 128.

Athaliah, 111.

Augustine, 2.

BAAL, 55.

Baasha, 109.

Babel, signification of name, 40.

Babylon captured, 159.

Babylonian Shemites, migration of, 43.

Bacchides, 167.

Balaam, prophecy concerning the Messiah, 70 sq.

Bamôth, 127.

Baptism of Jesus, 185 sq.

Baruch, 130.

Bathsheba, 89.

Baumgarten, Michael, 45, 196.

Baur, F. C., 197.

Bengel, 148.

Benjaminitish kingdom, failure of, 84.

Bethlehem-Ephratah, 78, 121.

Blood, medium of atonement, 66, 143.

Buddeus, J. F., 2.

CAIN, 30 ; his wife, 32.

Caius Popilius Lænas, 154.

Cambyses, 151.

Carcase, disposition of, 65.

Carchemish, 128.

Celano, 127.

Chanucca festival, 161.

INDEX II.

REFERENCES TO THE SCRIPTURES AND APOCRYPHA.

—o—

OLD TESTAMENT.

APOCRYPHA.

NEW TESTAMENT.

THE END.

MORRISON AND GIBB, EDINBURGH,
PRINTERS TO HER MAJESTY'S STATIONERY OFFICE.